**My heartfelt thanks to**
Simone Lacroix, Madeleine Limet and Marguerite
Begon, to Jacqueline Begon, my mother, to Pierre Coumont, my father,
and to everyone with a passionate interest in good but simple food
who inspired and supported me and who sometimes sowed seeds of
doubt in my mind, thus enabling me to forge ahead and try to fulfill my
vocation as an inveterate proponent of 'real food'.
Alain Coumont

And, from the bottom of my heart, thanks to all who, day by day,
make our daily bread what it is.

I first met Alain Coumont in 1999, when he was opening New York City's second Le Pain Quotidien, in SoHo. A mutual friend of ours from Brussels, an art collector, had suggested I seek him out because of his reputation in Belgium as a food visionary.

As I walked through the doors of 100 Grand Street, a man carefully applying plaster to the walls looked down from his ladder to greet me—Alain. We sat at one of the restaurant's communal tables and began to talk about his experience as a chef in Brussels and his hopes for Le Pain Quotidien in New York.

In 2003, I joined Le Pain Quotidien as Chief Executive Officer, charged with taking Alain's vision of offering simple, wholesome food in a convivial, authentic atmosphere and guiding its development into a successful international business.

Since then, I have had the pleasure and the privilege of expanding the company across continents, partnering with exceptional operators who remain true to the vision, and getting to know Alain even better.

*Alain Coumont's Communal Table* is a glimpse into Alain's passion for creating delicious and healthy recipes while exploring progressive ways of thinking about food. In reading his stories, you will travel with Alain through the formative moments that brought him from his aunt's kitchen to the founding of a restaurant concept that now welcomes guests in more than 100 locations across the globe.

At the communal table in SoHo, Alain introduced me to a restaurant concept and a lifestyle that have become a significant part of my daily life. To me, Le Pain Quotidien represents a return to simplicity and to our traditions. Sharing wholesome food around the communal table serves as a reminder that we are all connected — to each other, to the planet, and to life itself.

Le Pain Quotidien as we know it today would not be possible without the dedication of our team: the bakers, restaurant staff, support teams and franchise partners.

I thank them for bringing so much of themselves to our table. They are the backbone of our company — our *pain quotidien* — and both Alain and I are grateful for their energy and spirit.

I hope you enjoy learning Alain's story and exploring some of the wonderful recipes he shares in the coming pages.

Welcome to our family,

Vincent Herbert
New York, NY
August 2009

Text and photography *Jean-Pierre Gabriel*

Recipes *Alain Coumont*

Graphic design and typesetting *Oeyen en Winters*

Translation *Laura Macilwaine*

Made by *Albe De Coker NV.*

© 2009 Editions Françoise Blouard, Jean-Pierre Gabriel and Alain Coumont

D/2009/10.612/3

ISBN 978-2-87510-015-3

EAN 9782875100153

www.francoiseblouard.com

www.lepainquotidien.com

# A 'sweet-toothed', hunky-dory childhood

I was born in Huy, a small town on the river Meuse in southern Belgium. My parents had a grocery store in the town, on the corner of rue des Fouarges and rue des Rôtisseurs. My father had trained as a chef at the hotel management school in Namur. But as my grandfather had fallen ill, he had been forced to give up on the idea of pursuing any personal plans that he might have had and to take over the family business and support his mother instead.

The life story of my grandfather, Fernand Coumont, is quite extraordinary and reflects an entire era in itself.

François, my great grandfather, was a manservant in a country house in the region. He had been given a small plot of land as a kitchen garden, on which he grew vegetables. When he was nine or ten years old, my grandfather used to walk to the market in Huy, the nearest town, with a cart drawn by a dog. Together they made a 30-kilometre round trip to sell the vegetables grown in the kitchen garden at Huy market. When my grandfather grew up he became more professional. He met Madeleine, my grandmother, and bought a small store in Huy. It was his first grocery and he was what used to be known as a costermonger, a sort of street merchant. He had a cart, horse-drawn this time, and went round farms. He collected butter and cheeses, poultry and game, eggs, potatoes, honey, fruit and anything in fact which he could sell in town.

A little later, one of his cousins, an industrialist from Brussels by the name of Lallemand, bought a fine property, a former bank, in Huy, and rented it cheaply to my grandfather. We lived in the apartment above the grocery store. So it could be said that I was born with a silver spoon in my mouth.

I remember the cellar. It had been the strong room. When the bankers left, the safes had been removed and the gaping alcoves had been turned into storage areas for cans. Each alcove had its speciality: litre-size cans of peaches next to half-litre cans, canned tomatoes, concentrates, etc.

As far as his father's business sense is concerned, my father recounts an amusing anecdote. It happened during World War Two, when the German occupiers were printing paper money to pay their soldiers. I have never known how or why my grandfather smelt a rat and realized that once the war was over this paper money would be worth much less. But he asked his customers to pay for their eggs, lettuces, etc., in coins only!

As the currency was indeed devalued, paper money was replaced, but not coins. It would have been far too expensive for the country. I believe it took my grandfather ten years to dispose of all the coins which he had accumulated. All his suppliers were paid in coins. Every evening, the family went down to the cellar to fetch a bucket of coins, then used newspaper to make 'twists' of 5 centime, 10 centime, 20 centime coins. My father and my uncle tell how when they were kids, there were heaps of coins piled high and how they used to amuse themselves by jumping into them, like sand dunes.

My father took over the family business in the 1960s. The Golden Sixties. He went upmarket, raising the standard of quality and extending the range. Twice a week, he drove an ancient red Chevrolet truck to Brussels to buy vegetables at the early morning market. His gods were the buyers for Rob, the luxury grocery store in Brussels. They had large baskets inscribed with 'Rob' in gold lettering. They were the lords of the early morning market. The finest and most expensive produce was for them. That made a big impression on my father. When he took over the family business, he used Coumont 'the fresh produce specialist' as a slogan, copying it from Rob. Nowadays, people copy slogans from London or Milan. At the time, Brussels was almost like a foreign country. My father really did raise standards; he started selling foie gras, small packs of caviar and truffle peel and  installed a fish tank with live lobsters in the store. That's the background.

Women first got me interested in cooking. Marguerite Begon, my maternal grandmother, was a cook. She and René, my grandfather, kept a hotel and restaurant opposite the north station in Huy, as was often the case in medium-sized towns at the time. Unsurprisingly, it was called Hôtel du Nord. The café-restaurant was called Le Cap Nord. I can still see my grandmother in her kitchen. To me, as a child, it seemed huge. And in fact, probably was.

There were six Nestor Martin gas stoves in a row, fuelled by 4-burner gas cylinders, so there were a total of 24 gas burners. She also used Tefal™ frying pans – domestic rather than truly professional kitchen utensils. She was a workaholic. My grandparents never went abroad, in fact I don't think that they ever even ventured as far as the North Sea coast in Belgium. With the train station opposite their house and in a country as small as Belgium, it seems incredible. But that's how it was.

It's somewhat paradoxical but it was not really with her that I learned to cook. There was also my paternal grandmother and, even more importantly as things turned out, Aunt Simone. We called her aunt but she was in fact the mother-in-law of my uncle, my father's brother. She lived in the country with her husband, who was the station master of Moha, a tiny village in the region.

They grew potatoes and kept poultry and rabbits. She made her jams with fruit from the garden, going to the farm to collect her milk every morning. I remember that she boiled it before putting it in the refrigerator.

Every Saturday she baked 12 to 15 tarts. And every Sunday, the entire family came to drink bowls of coffee and eat rice tart, gooseberry tart and pound cake waffles!

She also did a lot of home-preserving, using Weck™ canning jars. There were preserved beans, tomatoes, plums, cherries and the like.

So it was really with Aunt Simone that I learned to cook. When I was two or three years old, she used to stand me on a chair while she was making her pastry. It was pâte levée sucrée (sweet bread dough) that she rolled out. She put it on round baking tins and snipped the edges off with her rolling pin. I used to make little apple turnovers with these scraps of dough.

That was why sweet things appealed to me, like any child who likes sweets and candies.

After this fruit tart phase, when I was six or seven years old I started to read. There were only two cookbooks at home. The first book was of the domestic, rudimentary kind, a free gift with the purchase of a pressure cooker. The second was one my father received from the hotel management school when he was awarded a prize as the best dining room student. It was a thick cook book published by Flammarion and entitled *L'Encyclopédie de la Gastronomie française* (Encyclopaedia of French Gastronomy).

All the recipes were illustrated with photos, but everything was classic, with mayonnaise, mimosa poached eggs, served on long oval dishes called torpedo dishes! I taught myself to cook with this book, reading recipes and hints. I started by making chocolate mousse, cream puffs and éclairs. I had a sweet tooth until I was 13 or 14, as far as I can remember. Before that age I was never tempted by anything savoury.

# From flour to sourdough starter bread

*Larousse gastronomique* says that in baking, this concept refers to 'sour dough', used to leaven bread. Every day the baker has to 'refresh' his levain (sourdough), by kneading it with flour and water. He uses part of it that day and keeps the other half, the chef (dough-like starter), to repeat the same operation the next day.

According to The Oxford Companion to Food, there are three stages in the creation of a levain (sourdough). First, a basic mix is prepared. In its simplest form it is a dough made from flour and water, providing food and moisture for the yeast spores which the baker hopes are present. When this mixture is fermented, part is used to make a bake of bread rise.

Bread forms part of the family of living and evolving foodstuffs whose special flavour, personality and individuality appeal to us. Bread is a product of fermentation, like cheese, yogurts and kefirs, beer, wine and cider, to name but a few. Fermentation is dependent on the action of micro-organisms, living things which convert the sugars contained in the raw materials, generating in the process a whole range of aromas and flavours characterizing a finished product, expressing its terroir; its place of origin in the broadest sense, in a word, giving it its unique personality.

There is naturally a great temptation to channel, standardize and dominate this process and thus to create uniformity.

Wine and its vinification provide a telling example of the difference which can exist between total control, industrialization of fermentation and making good use of the yeasts found naturally on the surface of grapes.

Roughly the same rules apply to bread and bread-making and the same trends are apparent. Baker's yeast, an industrial product, has largely superseded the sourdough variety, a change which occurred on a massive scale during the twentieth century.

Things were quite different for thousands of year, since the day when a small piece of dough which a baker had forgotten about produced a different kind of bread. The dough, which had been left in the open air, had swollen, becoming more elastic and spongy.

It has since been learned that this change in texture is the culmination of a process involving two successive stages. During the first stage, an enzyme called amylase converts the starch in the flour into maltose, a sugar consisting of two linked glucose units.

As they now have food available, the agents responsible for fermentation can get to work and convert the sugar into alcohol (ethanol) and carbon dioxide. The bubbles given off by the carbon dioxide cause the dough to swell and consequently create the cavities which make its texture lighter and spongy.

Without wishing to describe the whole of the living process of bread-making, one of the main players, the keystone, so to speak, of the process which gives the dough its plasticity, needs to be mentioned here. It is a substance which the Chinese very accurately describe as the 'muscle of flour', namely gluten.

It is thanks to the action of the gluten proteins – combined with the water incorporated into the dough – that the dough has a degree of elasticity, which allows pressure to be put on the lump of dough to flatten it, after which it gradually returns to its original shape.

In terms of pure physics, the gluten weaves a network of proteins which give dough its expansion capacity through the action of carbon dioxide bubbles.

These purely technical phenomena occur in roughly the same way, whether baker's yeast or sourdough starter is used.

# From flour to sourdough starter bread

The success of sourdough starter is also dependent on regularity. From the first to the last day, morning and evening, the starter dough comes into contact again with the flour, water and salt, to 'refresh' it, leading to a sort of permanent rejuvenation.

All the ingredients of the sourdough starter are used at 'room temperature'. The optimum temperature at which the starter dough will rise is 27-28°C.

If one is interested in the flavour of things, in sensations appealing to the taste buds, in food which is eye-catching and smells delicious, making life more pleasurable and love of eating a virtue, in short, if one is interested in the soul and essence of food, then one should take the time to nurture sourdough starter, as Steven L. Kaplan so aptly puts it. To paraphrase his description, sourdough starter is made from wild yeasts and bacteria present in the raw materials or the ambient air of the bake house. It is perpetuated by systematic successive 'refreshment' (or enrichment), ensuring selection and reproduction of the flora, consisting primarily of a combination of its acidifying bacteria and its own yeasts. Dough made using a sourdough starter produces bread whose cream-coloured texture is considerably denser, more irregular, supple and elastic than bread made using baker's yeast. Its crust is thicker. It naturally keeps better. It prides itself on being more nutritious because it is richer in vitamins and certain enzymes.

However, making good bread without the right type of flour is impossible. Whether used to make sourdough starter yeast or bread – wheat or rye – the flour used by Le Pain Ouotidien is always stone-ground. Stones grind the flour more finely than metal cylinders, the corollary being that the bran particles are smaller in size. The presence of bran particles means that bread made with stone-ground flour has a more pronounced flavour, evocative of crunchy whole cereal grains.

By the same token, the germ is also more atomized, making its separation from the ground cereal more difficult. With its high oil content (these oils also being essential to the proper rising of the bread), the germ enhances the flour's nutritional value. The downside is that these fatty substances ultimately cause the flour to go off more quickly. Stone-ground flour's shelf-life is therefore limited to a few months.

# Le Pain Quotidien's sourdough starter

**To produce a sourdough starter, the following are required**

a total of 2kg of stone-ground whole wheat flour,
1.2 litres of spring water
and grey (i.e. unrefined) salt.

The creation of a sourdough starter is an investment where patience is key. Starting from wheat flour, water and salt – the ingredients in the sourdough bread baked by Le Pain Quotidien – a fermentation process is set in motion, reaching its climax on the eleventh day.

- **The first day**

In the morning: in an earthenware or stainless steel bowl, quickly mix by hand 100g of flour, 60g of spring water and a pinch of salt. Cover with a plate and leave at kitchen temperature.

In the evening: 12 hours later, add 100g of flour, 60g of water and a pinch of salt, then mix quickly and cover with a plate.

- **The second day**

In the morning: keep only 150g of dough and add to it 100g of flour and 60g of water, mix quickly, cover and keep at room temperature.

In the evening: 12 hours later, keep only 150g of dough and add 100g of flour, 60g of water and a pinch of salt, then mix quickly and cover with a plate.

- **From the third to the tenth day**

In the morning and the evening, repeat the second day's operations.

On the morning of the eleventh day, start on the last stage.

- **The eleventh day**

In the morning the bread is kneaded for the first time. Take all the sourdough starter (310g) and add 500g of flour, 300g of water and a pinch of salt. Mix and leave to rest for 5 hours.

It takes 5 hours for the dough to acquire the status of ready-to-use starter yeast. By that point its total weight has increased to 1110g.

# Sourdough wheat bread

The use of steam is fundamental in the crust formation process, which conditions the texture of the inside of the loaf. In a dry atmosphere, the crust quickly solidifies, becomes airtight and prevents the gases from escaping. But these gases are what contribute to the formation of cavities in the bread, guaranteeing its elasticity and relative lightness. Steam helps to prevent the crust being formed from dying out and to keep it permeable for longer, until the loaf has reached its optimum size. Hence its importance.

**Makes two 2kg round loaves (weight after baking):**

720g sourdough starter,
2.5kg stone-ground flour (type 85),
1.75 litres filtered water or spring water,
40g unrefined sea salt.

- Ensure that all the ingredients are at a temperature of 25°-27°C. Put them all in the food processor bowl and, using the dough hook, knead at low speed for 3 minutes, then at high speed for 2 minutes and finally at slow speed for 5 minutes. Leave to rest in the bowl at a temperature of 27°-28°C for an hour and a half.
- Stir and compress the dough every 15 minutes by whizzing the hook for 3 seconds. This operation is therefore carried out six times, giving more body to the dough.
- To make two 2kg loaves, separate the dough into two 2.3kg lumps. Place them on a floured worktop (counter). This is when the proper process of making the bread begins. First of all, the lumps of dough need to be flattened to a thickness of 7-8cm, by literally 'boxing' the centre. Then stretch the dough to its four corners (think of the four cardinal points of a compass), then fold back each point to the centre of the lump.
- Repeat the operation at the four intermediate points (which would be the north east, south east, south west and north west here). Press firmly with the palm of the hand or the fist in the centre, to ensure that the eight points are sealed. Pick up the lump of dough and turn it over (top to bottom and vice versa), then put it into a well floured linen-lined bread basket.
- Cover with a clean cloth and leave to rest at a temperature ranging between 26°C and 28°C. Leave to 'proof' for between 3 1/2 and 4 1/2 hours depending on fermentation activity and the desired degree of acidity.
- The longer the dough is left to rest, the greater the acidity.
- Meanwhile, wrap up the remaining dough in a plastic bag and refrigerate for a few days, until the next bread-baking session.
- Just before baking, turn the dough in the bread basket out onto the stone hearth of an oven which has been preheated to a temperature of 240°C.

An oven with a stone hearth is essential for this type of bread. If you do not have one in your oven, look for a 4-5cm thick heat-resistant slab of stone, which may be lava stone, refractory brick, granite and the similar stones.

The small 200g lump which has been refrigerated will be the starter for the sourdough culture which may be made several days later. To do so, take this piece of dough out of the refrigerator. Return it to room temperature under a clean cloth, then add 330g of flour and 2dl of water. Mix and wait for 5 hours to produce the starter which will enable two further 2kg loaves (or four 1kg loaves) to be made.

- Using a razor blade, make one or more criss-cross marks on the surface of the lump of dough, thus adding the 'baker's signature'.
- At this point, ensure that there is a source of steam either by placing a small dish of hot water at the bottom of the oven or by spraying the surface of the bread and the burning stone, using a spray bottle, just before closing the oven again.
- Bake the bread for around an hour and ten minutes, to obtain a loaf weighing 2kg, showing a golden brown firm crust.
- Leave to rest for a few hours at least before slicing. Sourdough bread of this kind takes 2-3 days to mature properly, depending on the season and the atmosphere.

# Roasted hazelnut
## and raisin flûtes

For this type of bread, as for the baguette à l'ancienne, use of sourdough starter is more a question of adding taste than of raising the dough. Its combination with baker's yeast enables the proportion of sourdough starter required to be reduced. If sourdough starter alone is used to raise such small amounts of dough, the time needed for the fermentation process to be completed will be longer than with baker's yeast, leading the surface of the lumps of dough to dry out.

**Makes 12 flûtes
(small and thin French
sticks):**

720g sourdough
wheat bread dough,
360g raisins (Smyrna variety),
360g whole hazelnuts,
50g water,
1g dried or 3 g fresh yeast,
1 tsp salt.

- Ensure that all the ingredients are at the room temperature of the kitchen.
- Arrange the hazelnuts in a single layer in a hot non-stick frying pan and toast them for a few minutes. Transfer to a dish and leave to cool.
- Preheat the oven to its maximum temperature. Put the ingredients into a large bowl and knead with both hands, so that everything is thoroughly mixed together. Divide into 120g lumps of dough.
- Place them on a floured worktop (counter) and using floured fingers, form into cylinder shapes measuring approximately 25cm in length.
- Let them proof (raise) for 1 1/2 hours covered with a sheet of plastic wrap at room temperature (26-28°C).
- Bake in a very hot oven preheated at 250°C for 15-20 minutes until they have turned a nice golden colour. (Place a small dish with 1 cup boiling water on the bottom of the oven to generate steam.)

# Baguette à l'ancienne (old fashioned)

Given the size of domestic ovens, make half-baguettes (225g lumps of dough) in the same way.

This dough is also suitable for regular bread baked in rectangular metal tins (pans). 'Proving' time will be longer (approximately 45 minutes).

**For the sourdough:**
100g flour (type 65),
65g water,
1g salt,
2g fresh baker's yeast.
The day before, prepare a sourdough with the baker's yeast. Quickly mix these ingredients, put in a bowl covered with a clean cloth, then leave at kitchen temperature for a minimum of 12 hours.

**For the dough:**
165g sourdough,
1kg flour (type 65),
650g water,
18g salt,
10g fresh baker's yeast
or 3 g of active dry yeast

- Put the water, the yeast, the sourdough and the flour into the food processor bowl and blend at slow speed with the dough hook for 1 minute.
- Add the salt, knead at medium speed for 3 minutes, turn off.
- Scrape the sides of the bowl with a plastic spatula to remove any lumps and knead at low speed for a further 4 minutes.
- Leave the dough to rest in the bowl for an hour and twenty minutes, whizzing the hook for 3 seconds every 20 minutes, or 4 times during resting time. The purpose is to stir and compress the dough, to give it more body. Take the dough out of the bowl and put it on a lightly floured worktop (counter).
- Cut into four 450g lumps, quickly roll them in the flour and leave to rest for 5 minutes.
- Carefully stretch the lumps of dough lengthwise with hands and the working surface still floured, to produce 40cm long 'baguettes'. This involves pressing the sides while rolling and making to-and-fro movements.
- Place the shaped lumps of dough on a large clean cloth, also floured. Fold the cloth between each baguette, so that they do not touch one another. Cover with a plastic sheet (not plastic wrap) and leave to 'prove' for approximately 25-35 minutes, depending on room tempera-
- ture. The hotter it is, the more quickly the bread will rise, and
- vice versa. Preheat the oven and the baking tray (place a small dish with 1 cup boiling water on the bottom of the oven to
- generate steam). Carefully place the lumps of dough on a floured baking tray, one at a time. The tray must be thin and the size of the lumps of dough. Using a razor blade, make 5 incisions, obliquely and slantwise. The blade must be at an
- angle. Place in the oven on the baking stone. Bake at 240°C for approximately 20 minutes, until the bread has turned a nice colour.

# Ten-seed whole cereal bread

Small individual loaves can also be made by weighing out 80-100g 'lumps' of dough. In that case, baking time is shortened to 25 minutes (at 250°C). Store them in a cool place.

Whole cereal (grain) bread can be eaten as it is or toasted when taken out of the refrigerator. It is absolutely delicious spread with butter and sea salt.

**Makes 2 loaves:**

100g pearl barley,
100g millet,
100g quinoa,
100g oat grains or flakes,
100g kamut,
100g buckwheat,
100g round rice
from the Camargue,
100g rye flour,
50g sunflower seeds,
25g sesame seeds,
25g linseeds,
15g Guérande grey salt,
75g dried sourdough starter
or 200g fresh sourdough
starter,
1 litre water,
1 tbsp virgin sunflower oil
(to grease the moulds).

- Weigh the 7 cereals and mix them in a large bowl. Remove 300g and crush finely in a vegetable mill or food processor.
- Mix the crushed cereals with the rye flour, salt, linseeds, sunflower and sesame seeds. Set aside.
- Moisten the remaining 500g of cereals with the litre of water (20°C) and leave to soak at room temperature for 48 hours.
- Two days later, drain to remove the soaking water which has not been absorbed on the crushed cereals, add the powdered sourdough starter and mix thoroughly. Add the soaked cereals, mix and leave to rest in the bowl for an hour.
- Preheat the oven to 250°C.
- Mix the contents of the bowl and transfer to two non-stick lightly greased rectangular moulds. Cover the upper surface of each lump of dough with a rectangle of lightly greased baking paper.
- Bake at 250°C for 20 minutes, reduce the temperature to 150°C and bake for a further 30 minutes. Leave to cool in the moulds for 3 hours.
- Turn out of the moulds and wrap the loaves in plastic wrap or put them in a Tupperware™ container. Store in a cool place for at least 24 hours before eating.
- Slice thin with a sharp, smooth-bladed knife which has been lightly greased beforehand.

# Gluten-free whole cereal petits lingots (lingot-shaped mini-loaves)

Like all bread, these petits lingots can be frozen. They can be removed from the freezer and easily brought back to the right temperature if they are toasted twice.

A large loaf can also be baked. To do so, follow the baking instructions in the recipe for whole cereal bread (previous pages).

Another less common gluten-free 'cereal' is amaranth, a plant typically grown in Latin America. It can be used to supplement the mix of cereals in this recipe.

**For 20 mini-loaves:**
200g whole millet,
200g quinoa,
200g buckwheat,
200g round rice from the Camargue,
50g sunflower seeds,
50g sesame seeds,
50g linseeds,
50g pumpkin seeds,
20 g sodium bicarbonate (also called baking soda),
1 litre spring water,
10g Guérande grey salt,
1 tbsp virgin sunflower oil (to grease the moulds).

- Two days ahead, mix together the four gluten-free cereals in a large bowl. Take 300g of this mixture and grind it finely in a vegetable mill or food processor bowl.
- Mix the ground cereals with the salt and the oilseeds (linseed, sunflower, sesame and pumpkin seeds). Set aside.
- Moisten the remaining 500g of cereals with the litre of water (temperature: 20°C). Leave to soak at room temperature for 36-48 hours.
- Two days later, heat the oven up to 250°C.
- Drain off the juice which has not been absorbed by the cereals left to soak and pour it over the ground cereals. Add the baking soda and mix thoroughly.
  Add the soaked cereals. Mix well and fill lightly greased non-stick individual rectangular moulds.
- Bake in the oven at 250°C for 20-25 minutes. Leave to cool in the moulds for an hour.
- Remove from the moulds and eat the same day. Just before serving, toast the petits lingots so that they are warm and crispy.
- They may also be served with good quality slightly salted butter or a small dish of virgin colza or sunflower oil.

# Apple and cinnamon muffins

The muffins will keep for 24 hours at room temperature. They can also be frozen when they have cooled. If they are not eaten within 6 hours of coming out of the oven, it is always preferable to warm them in a toaster or microwave oven for 10-15 seconds on normal power.

To help them keep their colour and to extend their shelf life, dried fruits are often treated with sulphur dioxide. Opt for organic products or products certified sulphur-free.

**Makes 12 muffins:**

220g organic dried apples
420g farine de blé bise (semi-wholemeal wheat flour),
400ml apple juice,
140ml water,
100ml soy or sunflower oil,
150g agave syrup or honey,
20g baking powder,
10g ground cinnamon,
1 whole egg,
5g salt,
neutral oil to grease the muffin tins

**For the topping:**

2 Granny Smith apples,
2 tbsp honey or agave syrup.

- Finely dice the dried apples.
- Mix the diced apple with the water and leave to rest at room temperature for at least an hour.
- Preheat the oven to 180°C.
- In a large mixing bowl, mix together the flour, baking powder, cinnamon and the salt. Set aside.
- In a separate mixing bowl, whip together the apple juice, agave syrup (or honey), egg and the oil. Ensure that the syrup (or honey) is properly dissolved into the mixture.
- Pour the wet ingredients onto the flour mixture and mix quickly with a wooden spoon to produce a smooth paste.
- Gently fold in the rehydrated apple.
- Using a pastry brush, lightly grease the muffin tins and divide out the mixture into the cups.
- Wash and core the Granny Smith apples, keeping the skins on, and then cut each apple into 12 slices. Put the pieces into a large mixing bowl and mix with 2 table-spoons of agave syrup or honey.
- Decorate each muffin with 2 thin strips of apple and bake at 180°C for 12-14 minutes.
- When the muffins have been removed from the oven leave them to rest for 5 minutes before turning them out onto a cake rack.

# Ricotta muffins

Grated Parmesan cheese, a fromage à pâte persillée (blue-veined cheese) or even feta can be substituted for half of the cheese in this recipe.

Agave syrup, called 'nectar' in Mexico, is made from the juice of the blue agave plant (Agave tequilana). The sap is extracted from the core of the plant when it is at least seven years old, then filtered and heated at a low temperature (under 45°C), which means this sweetener, which has a high fructose content, is regarded as a raw food.

**Makes 12 muffins:**

220g ricotta,
110g full fat sour cream or full-fat fromage blanc,
110g whole milk,
110g sunflower oil,
330g flour,
6g baking powder,
175g grated Gruyère, Emmenthal or Comté cheese,
25g finely chopped chives,
4 eggs,
12g salt,
1/2 tsp freshly ground black pepper,
neutral oil for the muffin tins.

**For the blueberry coulis:**

200g blueberries (fresh or frozen),
75g agave syrup,
1 tbsp lemon juice.

- Heat the oven to 180°C.
- In a large mixing bowl, mix together the ricotta, sour cream, milk, oil, eggs, salt and pepper using a spatula. Ensure that a smooth and creamy mixture is produced.
- In a separate bowl, mix together the flour and the baking powder. Gently blend the ricotta into the mixture with a wooden spatula.
- Add the grated cheese and the chives. Mix well and fill the pre-greased muffin tins with the mixture.
- Bake at 180°C for 12-14 minutes.
- When the muffins have been removed from the oven leave them to rest for 5 minutes before turning them out onto a cake rack.
- Blend the blueberry coulis ingredients and serve in a sauceboat.

# Organic buckwheat
## rawnola crunola

This rawnola crunola can be served with organic soy, rice or almond milk.

As all the components of this rawnola crunola are raw and organically grown, it should be put into a sealed bag and frozen if it is to be kept for any length of time. Germinated buckwheat seeds can also be dried in the sun for an afternoon or on top of a radiator overnight. Electric driers of the Ezidri type are another alternative.

**Serves 8-10:**

500g buckwheat,
100g dried whole small bananas,
50g linseed,
50g sunflower seeds,
50g pumpkin seeds,
50g currants or sultanas,
50g whole crushed almonds, quartered.

**Garnish to serve:**

1kg organic soy yogurt,
200g red berries (raspberries, wild strawberries, redcurrants, etc.),
8-10 mint leaves.

• Soak the buckwheat seeds in 2 litres of cold water for 15 minutes. Strain through a sieve and allow to germinate at room temperature for 48 hours, taking care to stir the seeds in the sieve. Rinse briefly after 24 hours and continue stirring regularly. When the germ begins to appear spread the seeds on metal trays.

• Preheat a fan-assisted oven to 50°C. Put the buckwheat into the oven and maintain this temperature until it has dried out completely (at least 3 hours.)

• Keep in a hermetically sealed jar.

• Dice the bananas into cubes (0.5cm on the side) and mix them with the dried buckwheat seeds.

• Combine all the ingredients together and serve with 100g of soy yogurt per person, a few red berries and a mint leaf.

# Apprenticeship

The turning point came in the USA. I was 15 and was spending the school holidays there as part of an exchange programme organized by a Belgo-American friendship association. My parents had had an American student as a house guest the previous year so they could send one of their children over to the USA the following year. It happened to be me.

I arrived at the McDonough family's home in East Greenwich next to Newport, Rhode Island in July 1976, the year of the USA's bicentenary. It was not very far from Boston or Cape Cod. They took me to Niagara Falls and to Washington DC. We went on a short trip to New York.

Then one day, while I was watching ABC on television in my room, I happened to see a long feature on Michel Guérard in Eugénie-les-Bains. He had been named 'Man of the Year' by Time Magazine. His photo was on the cover, with the title 'Hold the Butter'. His book, entitled *La grande cuisine minceur*, had been translated into English for the North American market under the title 'The Cuisine of Slimness' and had been a phenomenal success, becoming a best-seller. I was bowled over. When I had seen my grandparents working night and day, I had certainly not been attracted by their occupation. But this was something else – a totally different ball game.

When I returned home to Belgium, I said to my father: "I want to go to hotel management school". We went to Namur, but as it was already September 1 it was too late to enroll, so I had to wait a year. When I finally started, it was really funny because all the old teachers remembered my father.

That was the time when the adventure started. The first book I bought in 1978, at the beginning of my first year, was *La Cuisine gourmande* by Michel Guérard, which had just been published in France by Robert Laffont. That is where I discovered the world of savoury food.

I spent four years at the hotel management school in Namur. When I turned 18 and had learned to drive, I started to cook for people at weekends. My parents had organized a takeaway department in their store but there was no catering service as such for private receptions. As customers often asked about home catering, my father told them that his son was a student at a hotel management school and could come and do the catering for them. So I started to cook meals for 12 in the homes of the town's dignitaries.

During the week I lodged in Namur. On Friday afternoons, I left the school at around 3 or 4 pm and got home at around 5:30 pm. I quite often had a meal scheduled for the evening. My father had prepared the order according to the menu. I went to people's homes and prepared everything in their kitchen, nothing having been set up in advance. I peeled vegetables, boned young pigeons and dissected pigs' trotters. It was always stressful. I generally took a pal from school with me to wait on tables. That's how we started, first in Huy, providing a catering service for two or three families. Then we 'went up' to Brussels.

I had 'inherited' a clapped-out car which had been mouldering in a garage. It was a Ford Taunus station wagon which had originally been white but was now no particular colour at all. The body was so rotten at the bottom that the exhaust fumes penetrated the interior. Summer and winter alike, the windows had to be left open, otherwise driver and passengers would have expired before they reached their destination.

I sometimes catered for 200 wedding guests and stuffed everything into the car. I had blue plates decorated with flowers, from a range which was being discontinued and which I had bought cheap. My mother had built up a stock of hundreds of Shell glasses. At the time, you received very nice glasses as a free gift every time you filled up your car with gas. And as there were several cars at home because we were a large family, the cupboards were stuffed full of these Shell glasses!

No one has hundreds of identical glasses. So we used Shell glasses at receptions in the homes of 'posh' people. I had bought a caterer's oven with foldaway handles, as on sedan chairs. So the oven, the gas cylinder, the plates, the Shell glasses and all the food were stuffed inside the car. The roof rack was also full. One day, when we arrived in Brussels, we realized that a crate of tomatoes and the crate of vegetables had fallen off somewhere along the highway! It was 9 pm. Looking out of the window, we saw that the neighbour had a vegetable garden. So we jumped over the wall and nicked some leeks from him. The funny thing is that like my father, I won a prize for cooking.

I still had one last work placement to do and I chose Scheveneels, the best patisserie in Liège at the time. I spent three months there. I stayed in Liège to work at Café Robert, on Boulevard de la Sauvenière. Robert Lesenne was renowned. He prided himself on his contacts in the trade. He had promised to put in a good word for me with Roger Vergé, the famous chef at the Moulin de Mougins restaurant on the French riviera. A dream come true, or almost. The months went by and still no news from Mr. Vergé. So I got out my smartest notepaper and wrote to all the great French chefs of the time, the Michelin three star chefs. With my résumé, I wrote a cover letter explaining why I wanted to work for them, which I photocopied 18 times. In the letter, I said that I was willing to work without pay for a year.

The extraordinary thing is that almost all of them replied, even if the answer was no. Just imagine what it's like for a young chef to open a letter embossed with the name of Paul Bocuse's restaurant.

To cut a long story short, I received three positive responses. First from Gérard Boyer in Rheims, then, at the same time, from Georges Blanc (La mère Blanc) in Vonnas and from Jo

Rostand (La Bonne Auberge) in Antibes. In spring 1982, I found myself in Vonnas, in the Rhône-Alpes region of France. Georges Blanc paid guys like me €80 a month and paid for our accommodation at the young workers' hostel in Vonnas. He had been attracted by a line in my résumé which said that the Liège patisserie was "… one of the best in the kingdom of Belgium!", so I found myself employed as a pastry chef. At the end of the season, he suggested that I stay and offered to promote me and give me a pay raise. As I wanted to move on, he asked me which restaurant interested me. I said I would like to work with Michel Guérard; he picked up the telephone and got me a job there, in Eugénie-les-Bains. So at the end of the winter, in around February 1983, I found myself working at Michel Guérard's restaurant in the beautiful spa town of Eugénie-les-Bains in southwest France. My first job there was pastries. In fact, chefs are definitely macho. Things are changing but most of the time they are not really bothered about desserts. In leading restaurants in the USA, for example, pastry chefs are often women.

I returned to New York at the end of the same year. In the meantime, I had been back to the USA twice with my school. The geography teacher organized school trips for pupils. In 1978, we spent three months in the south, travelling through Florida, Louisiana, Mississippi and Tennessee. In 1979, we went to California, New Mexico, Nevada and Colorado.

I was fascinated by the United States. Come to think of it, I don't know whether 'fascination' is the right word. Like many things in life, everything happens by accident. My father had been persuaded to buy land in Florida, like lots of Belgians in the 1960s.

My parents got a free trip to Florida and my father made Super 8 films. And it's true that when you see Miami like that for the first time, with canals, palm trees, huge house, huge cars… And my father said that even the hotel's cleaner drove to work in a Cadillac! Even when you're only 4 or 5 years old, you're wide-eyed with wonder.

Working for Michel Guérard was what got me headed for America. The restaurant closed for 3 or 4 months every winter. People regularly called, looking for young private chefs to cook during the winter in the Caribbean or in the mountains, for example. A Belgian pal was ending his second season at Eugénie-les-Bains. The previous winter, he had worked in Switzerland for Princess Ira de Fürstenberg. In late 1983, the same Ira de Furstenberg called this chef pal again and asked him to go to New York. Her partner's brother worked for an American bank in Switzerland. The president of the bank in New York had broken a leg when getting out of the bathtub and was wheelchair-bound. The Swiss staff wanted to send a private chef over as a gift for Thanksgiving. My pal had already found a job in California. He passed the phone to me and the first thing I was asked was: "How much do you want to earn?"

At the time, I was earning €350 a month for an 80-hour week. I asked for $2,000 a month and started at $1,500. Three weeks later, I found myself in a 800m² apartment on Fifth Avenue in New York, with a guy who was boss of a bank with a staff of 17,000. He was single, having been divorced five times, loved Dewar's Scotch Whisky and ate only meat and potatoes.

I worked for him for a year and a half. I came back to Belgium every six months to renew my…tourist visa. A year and a half later I went back to France, working for Alain Senderens in Paris for six or seven months. Then I did a two-week placement with Joël Robuchon, followed by a month in Milan with Gualtiero Marchesi, the first Michelin three star chef in Italian history.

Next I returned to the USA to work for the same banker. Three months later, I was 'poached' by a wealthy lady. Her father had started out as a messenger on Wall Street. Amongst other things, he had become the biggest shareholder in Columbia Pictures. At the time Forbes Magazine ranked them in sixth place amongst the wealthiest people in the USA.

My salary doubled. In 1985 and 1986, I earned $4,000 a month, with board and lodging and even a car thrown in as part of the package. I had never really earned any money in my life. When you have always been virtually penniless, you react in one of two ways. Either you blow everything or you are reluctant to spend anything. My reaction was not to spend, I never even bought myself a $50 pair of shoes. It never even occurred to me to spend anything above that amount.

I worked mainly in New York. They had an apartment with 23 members of staff. A chauffeur, 3 butlers, 2 women who were responsible only for doing the laundry and ironing and a French dressmaker who only did alterations. Hubert de Givenchy came to the house for fitting sessions. On those days there was a small dinner. It involved a huge amount of work for me and no expense was spared: foie gras, truffles, caviar. There were monthly butcher's bills of $7,000-8,000.

I sometimes cooked joints of roast beef and 6-rib racks. The lady of the house only ate the slice in the middle, which had to be very rare but hot. When I had carved the joint, she drank the blood escaping from the cooked meat, in a glass. Her husband ate the two very well cooked outer slices. There was 5kg of meat left for the staff.

She sometimes asked for hamburgers and hot-dogs. At the age of 23 and having worked for Michel Guérard, one cannot help thinking "What a comedown..." But then you become a bit more relaxed. I remember that one day she wanted me to make an Indian dish for her, crab-filled pancakes. I analysed the recipe and managed to adapt it in a way that I found fun. It helped me to produce dishes which I would never even have considered if I had been left to my own devices.

In winter, we spent every weekend in the Bahamas. Sometimes we were there for two weeks. They had a gigantic house at Lyford Cay on the island of Nassau. I had five local mamas to help me in the kitchen and go to the local market. They taught me how to add exactly the right amount of extremely hot chillies!

The maître d' was English. He was the Spencer family's former butler and claimed to have been involved in the upbringing of the future Princess Diana. My employer had hired him to recount anecdotes about Diana, the royal family and English high society. He was really talented in an over-the-top sort of way. He was the star of the society evenings. The guests came to enjoy my cooking but were much more interested in the show put on by this maître d' who had missed his calling as an actor. I remember a dinner given for Michael Caine's birthday, at which Sean Connery, Laura Ashley and Mr. and Mrs. Cadbury were guests. The cake was a duo of white and dark chocolate, dusted with bitter cocoa. When Michael Caine blew out his 50 candles, our super butler and his white dinner jacket were covered in cocoa!

In early 1987, I spent $2,000 on a round-the-world ticket from the Bahamas, with New York as the first stop. I took all my cases and left them in Belgium. Then I set out for Amsterdam, Bangkok and Sydney… on my own, with just a backpack.

# Bombe au chocolat

**Serves 6-8:**

400g plain dark chocolate,
60cl fresh whipping cream
(35% fat),
50g groundnut
or sunflower oil.

**For the almond biscuit
(cookie) disc:**

100g egg whites
(2-3 eggs according to size),
50g caster (superfine) sugar,
50g icing (confectioners')
sugar,
100g ground almonds,
1 tbsp flour.

**For the mould:**

butter, flour.

**For the finish:**

bitter cocoa.

**On the first day,**

- Preheat the oven to 160°C.
- Thoroughly mix the caster sugar and the icing sugar to ensure that the latter does not form lumps. Leave to rest.
- Mix the ground almonds with half the sugar and the tablespoon of flour.
- Whisk the egg whites until they are not too stiff, adding half the sugar towards the end. Blend the almond mixture into the egg whites without stirring too much.
- Grease and flour a 20cm non-stick mould. Turn it over to remove the excess flour.
- Pour in the almond biscuit mixture. Bake at 160°C for 20 minutes. Leave to cool on a wire rack.

**On the second day,**

- Line a hemispherical stainless steel or earthenware bowl with plastic wrap. In this bowl, the top of the chocolate mixture has to fit the diameter of the almond biscuit disc, i.e. 20cm.
- Melt the chocolate and the oil in a bain-marie. Heat to 50°C.
- Take the cream out of the refrigerator (it needs to be well chilled). Half whip it, until it barely holds in the whisk, like for Irish coffee. Add a third of the cream to the melted chocolate and mix with a flexible rubber spatula for 20 seconds. Add the rest of the cream and blend it in with the spatula, lifting the preparation.
- This process should take only 10 seconds. Pour this mixture into the bowl and place the génoise biscuit disc on top. Refrigerate overnight.
- Remove from the mould and take off the film. Dust with bitter cocoa.
- To slice, dip a sharp knife in hot water before cutting each slice.

# Lemon tart

Sablé pastry dough needs to be well chilled to make it easier to roll out. As it is comparatively fragile, the advice that the lump of dough be placed between two plastic sheets is sometimes given.

The purpose of lining with melted white chocolate a prebaked pastry base, later to be filled, is simply to create a thin waterproof film, preventing the baked pastry from becoming moist and consequently crumbly.

Any pastry left over can be stored, if carefully wrapped, for one or two weeks in the refrigerator or for a few months in the freezer. If the pastry has been frozen, bring it back to room temperature by leaving it in the refrigerator overnight.

**Serves 6-8:**
**For the sablé pastry:**
200g butter,
150g icing (confectioners') sugar,
1 egg white,
1 lemon peel,
60g flaked almonds,
1 pinch salt,
300g flour.

**For the cream:**
190g liquid fresh cream,
150g sugar,
15cl freshly squeezed lemon juice,
90g full-fat fromage blanc,
peel of 1/2 lemon,
2 whole eggs,
3 egg yolks.

**For the finish:**
30g white chocolate.

- Preheat the oven to 160°C.
- Put all the pastry ingredients, except the egg, into the food processor with the paddle attachment. Blend for 1 minute to produce a sablé pastry mixture. Add the egg and mix for a further 20 seconds.
- Form a ball with the dough and wrap in plastic wrap. Refrigerate for at least 2 hours.
- For one tart, allow 250-300g of well chilled pastry. Flour the working surface. Use a rolling pin to flatten the pastry until it is 4-5mm thick. Line a 22-24cm in diameter pie dish (tart pan) with a removable base with the pastry.  Cover the pastry with baking paper, fill with dried beans and bake blind at 160°C for 25 minutes.
- Take out of the oven, remove the beans and the paper and bake for a further 5 minutes to dry the pastry.
- Leave to cool and brush the inside of the pastry base with a thin layer of white chocolate melted in a bain-marie beforehand.

- Put all the ingredients of the lemon cream in a food processor bowl and blend. Whip for 20 seconds. Strain through a conical strainer to remove any lumps.
- Pour into a small thick-bottomed pan and heat up over a medium heat, stirring continuously with a wooden spoon until the mixture reaches 92-93°C. When the mixture starts to thicken, remove the pan from the heat while continuing to stir. Pour into the pastry base, still in its mould.
- Leave to rest on the table for 5 minutes, without moving or disturbing the tart. Carefully transfer it to the refrigerator for at least an hour.
- Ideally, the lemon tart should be eaten the same day.

# Pecan tart

Low-fat fromage frais can be used but full-fat cheese obviously produces a creamier result.

The mixture and the pecan nuts can be baked on their own, without a pastry base, in individual portions, in a ramekin dish, a Catalan cream custard mould or, even better, a lightly greased non-stick mould.
When baked, turn out of the moulds

Muscovado sugar is produced from whole, concentrated sugar cane syrup, which is then dried and not centrifuged. The word 'muscovado' comes from the Spanish word mascabado, meaning 'unrefined'. This type of sugar is therefore rich in a variety of minerals.

**Serves 6-8:**

125-150g net
pecan nuts (shelled),
1 sablé pastry base
(see recipe, page 50).

**For the filling:**

200g liquid fresh cream,
100g smooth fromage blanc,
2 eggs,
2 egg yolks,
100g muscovado sugar,
1 tsp natural vanilla extract.

- Preheat the oven to 200°C.
- Break the meat of the nuts into 4 lobes and arrange them in a single layer on the tart base.
- Put all the ingredients in the filling into a large bowl. Whip for 30 seconds, without causing the mixture to froth. Pour it onto the nuts.
- Bake first for 10 minutes at 200°C, then for a further 10 minutes at 140°C.

# Apple tartlets

Fructose can be substituted for sugar. As fructose is a more powerful sweetener than conventional sugar, it produces the same sweet taste but with fewer calories.

Virgin vegetable oil can also be substituted for butter, reducing the saturated fats content. If vegetable oil is used, the amount of flour in the almond cream preparation needs to be increased slightly (count 20g).

If you wish to prepare this recipe in advance, you can freeze the little tarts raw and bake them as and when required. They will of course take longer to bake.

Apples can be replaced with seasonal fruits, such as peaches or plums, halved and skin side facing down. Sprinkle with icing sugar so that the tartlets will be nicely coloured.

**Makes 6:**
3-4 Granny Smith or Golden Delicious apples, 30g icing (confectioners') sugar.

**For the almond cream:**
125g ground almonds,
125g sugar or fructose,
125g chilled butter, cubed,
pinch of salt,
1 tsp natural vanilla extract,
50g flour,
2 large eggs,
peel of 1/4 lemon,
juice of 1/2 lemon

- Put the almonds, sugar, butter, salt, flour, vanilla extract and lemon peel in the food processor bowl. Blend for 1 minute, using the paddle attachment, until the mixture is of the consistency of fine sand.
- Add the eggs and the lemon juice. Blend for a further 20 seconds. Set aside this almond cream – the future filling – in a bowl.
- Refrigerate for at least 30 minutes. This almond cream will keep for several days in the refrigerator.

- Preheat the oven to 175°C.
- Wash and wipe the apples. Cut into 8 quarters without peeling. Remove the pips (seeds) and their membranes.
- Place baking paper cups on a muffin tray. Fill them two-thirds full with almond cream. On the surface of the cream, place a few apple quarters. Dust with icing sugar and bake at 175°C for 20-25 minutes
- Serve at room temperature or slightly warm.

# Apricot tartlets

In season, add a few fresh lavender flowers to the almond cream, allowing one flower for 6 people.

**Makes 6:**
Almond cream
(see recipe, page 54),
12 apricots,
30g icing
(confectioners') sugar.

- Preheat the oven to 175°C.
- Place baking paper cups on a muffin tray. Fill them two-thirds full with almond cream.
- On the surface of the cream, place 4 good quality canned apricot halves or fresh apricot halves, ripe but firm. Dust with icing sugar and bake at 175°C for 20-25 minutes. You can also bake a large family-sized tart. If so, bake for 30 minutes, taking care to lower the heat if the surface is colouring too quickly.
- For more pronounced colouring, put the tartlets under the broiler for 1-2 minutes after baking.

# NY cheese cake

To remove from the mould, slide the wet tip (plunged into hot water) of the blade of a knife around the vertical sides of the mould. Turn out carefully and place on a large dish. Decorate with strawberries or raspberries and serve with a red berry coulis or a slightly runny jam or jelly.

**Serves 12:**

**For the cream:**
4 eggs,
2 egg yolks,
600g cream cheese (Philadelphia, Kiri or Saint Moret, for example),
250g sugar or fructose,
50g pastry flour,
1 tsp natural vanilla extract,
pinch of salt.

**For the biscuit base:**
12 Petit Beurre biscuits, crushed,
50g melted butter

- Preheat the oven to 200°C. Mix together the sugar, pinch of salt and flour. Sieve and put into the food processor with the beater. Blend with the cheese, whisking for 1 minute. Add the whole eggs, the egg yolks and the vanilla. Blend quickly to obtain a smooth and homogenous cream.

- To assemble: Take a high-sided round mould, grease lightly and place a disc of baking paper, cut to fit the size of the mould exactly, inside. Using a spatula, mix the crushed Petit Beurre biscuit crumbs with the tepid melted butter. Pour into the mould and press down firmly so that the base is uniformly covered. Pour the cheese cream into the mould and bake at a temperature of 200°C for 10 minutes. Lower the oven temperature to 140°C and bake for a further 35 minutes. Leave to cool for 30 minutes, then refrigerate for 12 hours, still in the mould.

# Carré du mendiant
# (dried fruit and nut squares)

Slicing this cake while it's frozen means that the squares are geometrically shaped, while the texture is soft and chewy. Once cut, store the squares in an airtight tin at room temperature.

The almond mixture can be flavoured with orange and lemon peel.

As a variant, this cake can be made with walnuts and coffee. To do so, add two tablespoons of very finely ground coffee to the mixture before baking.

For a 'healthy' variant, substitute fructose for regular sugar and you have a pastry which contains no cholesterol or glucose but is rich in dried fruit and nut oils.

**Serves 8:**
200g egg whites (6-7 eggs),
120g caster (superfine) sugar,
120g icing (confectioners') sugar,
200g ground almonds,
25g pastry flour (3 tbsp),
pinch of salt,
65g whole almonds, with the skin,
65g whole hazelnuts, with the skin,
65g walnuts,
80g black raisins,
25g pistachios or pine nuts.

- Preheat the oven to 190°C.
- Carefully mix together the caster sugar and the icing sugar. Thoroughly mix the ground almonds with half of the two sugars mixture, the flour and the pinch of salt.
- Whisk the egg whites until they are not too stiff, which should take 30 seconds. Then blend in the remainder of the sugars mixture.
- When the egg whites are ready, add the ground almonds-based mixture, blending quickly. The mixture should not be too smooth and homogeneous.
- Mixed together all the dried fruits and nuts and place them in a square baking tin (pan), covered with baking paper. The baking tin must be large enough to allow the dried fruits and nuts to form a regular, densely packed layer, so that the almond mixture will not drip through onto the bottom. If necessary, fill in any gaps with extra dried fruits and nuts.
- Carefully pour the almond mixture over the dried fruits and nuts, ensuring that they do not move. Smooth the mixture delicately using a spatula and bake at 190°C for 35-40 minutes.
- After taking out of the oven, leave to cool at room temperature for 20 minutes and freeze in the baking tin for 12 hours.
- Turn out of the mould and cut into neat squares, using a sharp knife.

# Red berry crumble

Crumble can easily be made outside the red berries season. To do so, freeze them in appropriate portions when they are at their peak in terms of ripeness and taste. Specialty food retailers also stock excellent frozen mixtures of red berries

**Serves 6:**
400-500g mixed red berries: blackcurrants, red currants, raspberries, blueberries, blackberries, etc

**For the crumble:**
24 Petit Beurre biscuits,
100g fructose,
1/2 tsp powdered cinnamon,
40g butter.

- Preheat the oven to 225°C.
- Roughly crush 12 Petit Beurre biscuits with a fork, then divide them out, in 6 small individual gratin dishes or 6 ramekin dishes.
- Place the mixed red berries on this first layer of biscuits.
- In a bowl, roughly crush the remaining 12 Petit Beurre biscuits with a fork. Mix them with the fructose, the cinnamon and the melted butter.
- Divide the mixture out in the dishes, above the fruit.
- Bake at 225°C for 15 minutes.

# Crème brûlée and caramel tart

**Serves 6-8:**

1 sablé pastry base
(see recipe, page 50).

**For the cream:**

50cl fresh cream,

4 egg yolks,

1/2 vanilla pod,

1 whole egg,

60g sugar.

**For the soft caramel:**

75g sugar,

75g fresh cream,

80g white chocolate.

- Preheat the oven to 110°C.
- Split the vanilla pod lengthwise. Scrape out the seeds with a small paring knife. Put in a small pan with the fresh cream and bring to a boil. Remove the vanilla pod.
- Break the whole egg into a large bowl, add the yolks and sugar and mix with a wooden spoon. Pour in the boiling cream in two stages. To avoid 'cooking' the eggs, first raise the temperature with a quarter of the cream. Mix with the spoon and add the rest.
- Strain through a conical strainer and pour onto the pastry base. Bake at 110°C for 15-20 minutes.
- Leave to rest at room temperature for 20 minutes, then refrigerate.
- Melt the 80g white chocolate in a bain-marie.
- Put the sugar in a frying pan, turn up the heat so that the dry heat caramelizes it, turning it light brown in colour. Lower the temperature by adding the fresh cream. When the mixture has cooled down and is tepid, add the white chocolate and whisk to produce a smooth and homogeneous caramel.
- Pour onto the well chilled tart to form a 3mm coating.
- Smooth and level out with a flat metal spatula

## Le Café du Dôme

At the end of my world tour, I came back to Belgium. I didn't want to go back to America. A private chef is a luxury slave. It's a well paid job but you can be woken up at 2 am and asked to make eggs and bacon.

You can't plan anything. Even when not working, you always have to be at the ready. It's almost like being a fireman in a firehouse. And another thing was that I was starting to get a bit fed up throwing out half-full 2kg cans of caviar.

I wanted to come back to Europe. After having lived in New York for four years, the thought of living in Huy again seemed challenging, let us say. I wanted to open a little restaurant in Brussels, with the idea of serving fine cuisine at reasonable prices, although setting it up should not involve large-scale investment.

During my years in the USA I had not needed to spend much. My board and lodging had been paid for. As I was more the squirrel type, I had saved enough money to imagine having my own establishment. So I walked around Brussels, doing my own survey, until one day I came across a 'For Rent' sign on the window of a restaurant on the corner of a down-at-heel street near the North Station. It was on the first floor of an antiquated hotel. I seem to remember that it may even have been called Le Cap Nord, the name of the restaurant owned by my maternal grandparents. Or else it was L'Etoile du Nord.

The atmosphere was very retro, full of nostalgia, and I remember the magnificent tiled floors. It was huge, with a very high, almost monumental ceiling. I really wanted to set up in business there.

My realtor had arranged a meeting with the owner of the building, a man called Arthur Vogel. With his business associates, he had bought up the whole district, in anticipation of the economic boom to which the development of the European institutions had indeed led. After proper refurbishment, the old hotel, for which they had paid €500,000, had been sold for €6.5 million.

They agreed to rent the restaurant to me but forced me to agree to enter into a partnership… and to use the services of their interior decorator.

I had no control over the renovation and refurbishment of 'my' restaurant. Given the sheer scale of the building work, it took six months just to get planning permission and twice as long to carry out the work.

I ended up with a monstrosity, a pseudo-Starck design commissioned by the Costes brothers, which had gone wrong – and in a big way. I had wanted to preserve the soul of the place but what I had got was mock modern and a mezzanine floor instead of the original high ceilings! In 1987, this renovation and refurbishment work cost €450,000. And the monthly rent – of €6,000 – was disproportionate to my initial plans.

All the time that the renovation work was going on, a total of 18 months, I was bored out of my mind. I had no job or income and I was eating into my savings. The best I could do was to bail myself out by catering for a few private functions.

At the beginning, I lived with my mother, who by then was separated from my father. So I had all the time in the world to brood. I wondered how I could make myself known when I had no recent career to my name in Belgium.

It was then that I came up with the idea of writing a cook book. It would be brought out to coincide with the opening of the restaurant and it would get press coverage. It was purely a marketing strategy.

I had met the Belgian publisher Vander at a function for which I had provided the catering service. I told him about my project. He was not interested in publishing the book but he was prepared to produce it as an author. He calculated that with a hundred photos, it would cost €17,500 to produce a print run of 5000.

I set about making a list of recipes. I needed a hundred, the same number of illustrations planned.

I didn't have a camera. My mother's uncle, a retired restaurateur who was in his eighties, happened to be president of the Camera Club of Andenne, a small town in our region. He lent me a fully manual Leica. By way of an automatic cell, there was an arrow which moved according to the light. In the space of two weeks during the summer, I took all the shots of the dishes that I cooked. A real one-man show!

My mother's garden was my studio. Her neighbour, a nuclear engineer, was mad about his kitchen garden and an early convert to everything organic. He grew a whole range of organic vegetables, including artichokes, tomatoes and asparagus. His garden was a dream come true for me, with every conceivable ingredient I could have wished for – and right next door!

When I had my photos developed, part of the roll of film had been scratched by the lab. It was a piece of bad luck but I still had some good photos all the same. It was then that I wrote the texts of the recipes, carefully looking at each photo so as not to leave out any ingredients.

As I was getting into marketing, I needed to find a theme, to make my book stand out amongst the cook books then being published on a mega scale. I didn't need to look far for inspiration. My father had had a heart attack at the age of 34. He had to take medication every day, a drug called trinitrine, to thin the blood. When I was a kid, I had had direct experience of his diet. Margarine was substituted for good old farm butter. I had put up a 'healthy eating' poster in my bedroom, a sort of pie chart showing all types of food with their protein and vitamin content, number of calories, etc.. The sort of posters which are to be found in drugstores and pharmacies.

I had found my hobby horse: it would be eliminating cholesterol from the diet. No butter, no sugar, no egg yolks. Only egg whites. I had a subject for my book, recipes and photographs and I was prepared to finance its publication on my own. I had even forked out €7,500 on photoengraving.

You can rush headlong into such a project. But you soon come to realise that you will need people to help sell it. It was then that I happened to meet the wife of Parisian publisher Jacques Legrand. She was Belgian, from Liège. She saw the manuscript and the photos and liked my work. She got me an introduction to one of her friends, one of the daughters of publisher Robert Laffont. That was how I got to meet Claude Joly who, under the name Claude Lebey, was responsible for publication of *Les recettes originales* series at Robert Laffont. Until then he had only published Michelin three star chefs, including Michel Guérard, author of the first cook book I had ever bought and my former boss. For my part, I had taken the initiative and had already written to Michel Guérard, asking him whether he would agree to write the preface to my book, and he had agreed.

Feeling confident, I drove to Paris in my small blue second-hand Opel Kadett car. I arrived at the publisher's offices with the Ektachrome films, the photoengraving of the pictures, the manuscript and Michel Guérard's letter. I met Claude Lebey's secretary. He himself granted me a two-minute interview in his office. I spent just one hour at Laffont, including the time it took to hand over my negatives and photos to the production manager. The following day, when I was back home, the telephone rang. It was Claude Lebey's secretary and, in substance, I was being asked to go back to Paris immediately.

This time, Claude Lebey and I had a meal together. He told me that I had his secretary to thank. She had read the manuscript, she liked it and the photos were fabulous. But there was a major problem. Lebey had taken the initiative of telephoning Michel Guérard – who had said that he longer wanted to put his name to the preface!

And no preface signed by Guérard meant no book.

Taking Claude Lebey's advice, I got back into my Kadett and headed for Eugénie-les-Bains. I slept on the spot, in a cheap hotel, costing something like €6 a night, which was dirt cheap, even at the time. The following day – it was a Sunday – I had an appointment at 11 am. I was shown into the piano room. Michel Guérard arrived. We talked a bit, he leafed through my manuscript and had it photocopied by his secretary.

Five minutes later his wife Christine arrived, accompanied by their lawyer, a Belgian living in Paris. As I had the bundle of photos, she looked at them and every other picture exclaimed: "But that's just like Guérard!"

My former boss ended the interview by saying that he regretted that he was unable to write the preface, although he congratulated me on the quality of the work.

I had just driven a thousand kilometres, I had been expecting to be on a high and instead I had been brought down to earth with a bump, with the words: "Sorry, it's just not possible. But be our guest. Stay for lunch." ringing in my ears. So at noon, I was shown to a table and was served the gastronomic menu and drank a bottle of claret, to myself. When it was time for coffee, around 2.30 pm, the maître d' came and told me that Mr and Mrs Guérard would like to see me in the garden.

There were still three of them, including their lawyer. All very nice. Michel Guérard spoke: "We've been thinking things over, you've done a really good job, but I'm not going to write the preface. Even better, I'm going to co-author the book." Then they started talking about the publishing contract amongst themselves. I seemed to be completely out of the picture, as if I were non-existent.

One of my mother's aunts, a former tax inspector, had retired to south west France, near the town of Cahors. I went to stay overnight at her house that evening. The following morning we visited the neighbours. I remember filling an empty Evian water bottle with their Cahors wine. I was so happy that I knocked back a litre and a half of rough Cahors wine from the vat while driving back to Belgium.

The book was published in the fall of 1989 and was entitled *Minceur exquise, 150 recettes pour maigrir en se régalant* (Exquisite slimness. 150 recipes to slim while eating well). Le Café du Dôme had been open for several months and naturally I had not been awarded a Michelin star.

To mark the book's publication Laffont had organized everything with consummate skill. The bosses of Moët & Chandon champagne had made their private jet available to us. We took off from Le Bourget airport in Paris one morning to fly to Pau, then travel on to Eugénie-les-Bains. On board were the crème de la crème of Parisian gastronomic journalists.

Michel and Christine Guérard received us for lunch. Then everyone, including Michel and Christine Guérard, who had joined the party, took the plane back to Brussels, for a dinner at Le Café du Dôme. Brigitte Forissier, Robert Laffont's press attaché for Belgium, had got out the troops, in the form of every single journalist around. My family and a few friends were also present. The restaurant was packed. By the time we got to the dessert, I had been kidnapped by Brigitte and was on my way to the studios of Belgian public television. I was guest of the day on the late night news of RTBF, the French-speaking channel. I was absolutely petrified. A publicity stunt had been my dream and I had certainly got one.

But this media launch was short-lived and not particularly productive. Under the partnership contract with the property developers, each party had a 50% stake. The contract also provided that should the building be sold, they would give me a cheque for €250,000. Instead, they sold me with the furniture, to get round the clause – which meant that they did not have to compensate me.

I then became a consultant for the new owners of the building, a Spanish chain, which paid me a monthly retainer of €2,500 for three years.

When that contract ended, I continued working in Brussels, in a new five-star hotel, the Stanhope, for the same unscrupulous speculators. This venture did not last long, just two months in fact. It was the first time in my life that I got fired.

That evening, the gastronomic critic of Gault et Millau, the famous French food guide, happened to be in the restaurant. I found out later that this dreaded critic had actually awarded us 15/20 ... Not bad for a newly established restaurant, especially in a hotel.

The restaurant had found its feet and was now up and running. It was going great guns. The general manager came and asked me to make a ham sandwich for a room service order, to be sent up immediately. He was putting me under pressure. I sent him packing, saying: "Do it yourself."

And I was fired.

# Lemon spéculoos

To keep these biscuits (cookies) fresh, they can be deep-frozen in a tightly sealed freezer bag and taken out of the freezer as required. Deep-freezing means that when removed from the freezer they are just as delicious as when freshly baked.

The pastry balls can also be deep-frozen and the spéculoos can be sliced and baked as required. This 'home' bake-off method results in incomparably fresh products.

**Makes 60:**
210g chilled butter,
300g pastry flour,
210g demerara sugar,
1 tsp powdered cinnamon,
pinch of small pieces lemon peel,
pinch salt,
1 egg,
juice of 1/4 lemon,
150g flaked almonds.

- The day before, put the butter (cut into cubes), flour, demerara sugar, cinnamon, lemon peel and salt into the food processor bowl. Using the paddle attachment, mix for approximately 30 seconds to produce a sablé (rich short crust/sugar crust) pastry mixture.
- Add the egg and the lemon juice and blend for 10 seconds. Transfer to a large mixing bowl and add the flaked almonds, mixing gently with a spatula to minimize breakage of the almonds. Place two sheets of alumin(i)um foil, 20-25cm long, on the worktop (counter). Place half of the pastry in the middle of each. Roll up the foil to form two regular sausage-shaped parcels. Refrigerate for at least 12 hours.
- The following day, preheat the oven to a temperature of 140°-150°C.
- Unwrap the pastry parcels and cut them into regular thin slices, 3-4mm thick. Place them on a baking tray covered with baking paper. Bake for approximately 12-15 minutes.
- Leave to cool for 10 minutes, then immediately transfer the spéculoos to an airtight tin (Tupperware™, for example) to ensure that they stay dry and crispy.

# Pistachio, olive oil and lemon peel biscotti

Biscotti – like the British English word 'biscuit', derived from old French, itself derived from Latin – literally means 'baked twice', which makes sense in this particular recipe.

Like glucose, fructose is present in fruit and honey. Chemically, they are both exactly the same. But the structure of their atoms is different. Fructose is metabolized by our bodies more slowly than other sugars. It is the sweetest of all the common sugars. In cold drinks – only – just half the amount is required to obtain the same sweetness as with 'normal' sugar, meaning that the calorie intake is lower. However, this remarkable sweetening power returns to normal in hot drinks. Opt for fruit fructose, as there is also fructose synthesised from glucose.

The use of virgin oil is designed to make these biscuits/cookies light and easily digestible.

**Makes 30:**
6cl extra virgin olive oil,
350g flour,
150g fructose,
2 whole eggs,
2g salt,
5g bicarbonate of soda,
180g green pistachios, unsalted and unroasted,
peel of one lemon,
peel of one orange,
3 tbsp lemon juice,
1 tbsp natural vanilla extract.

**For the finish:**
fructose

- Preheat the oven to 150°C. Put all the ingredients, apart from the pistachios, in the food processor bowl. Whip with the paddle attachment for 30 seconds. Transfer the dough to a large mixing bowl and add the pistachios.
- Knead the dough to blend in the pistachios. Form two 20cm-long sausage shapes and roll them in the fructose, so that they are covered by a crystal crust.
- Place them on a baking tray covered with baking paper. Flatten them slightly and bake for 35 minutes.
- Remove from the oven and leave to cool for 10 minutes. Cut the sausage shapes into oblique slices 15mm thick and return to the oven for 8-10 minutes to ensure that the biscotti dry out.

# Ginger snaps

The powdered ginger can be replaced by 20g of fresh ginger, cut into minute cubes.

If you want your biscuits (cookies) to be paler in colour, you can mix the types of sugar, using half muscovado and half caster (superfine) sugar.

**Makes 80:**

250g chilled butter,
875g pastry flour,
900g muscovado sugar,
4g powdered ginger,
2g powdered cloves,
2g powdered cardamon,
2g powdered cinnamon,
2g salt,
20g bicarbonate of soda,
5 whole eggs,
3 tbsp white wine vinegar.

**For the finish:**
coarse granulated sugar.

- Preheat the oven to 150°C. Put all the ingredients except the eggs and the vinegar into the food processor bowl and whip for 30 seconds. Add the eggs and vinegar and whip for a further 15 seconds.
- Remove the dough and put it into a mixing bowl. Mix with a spatula until it becomes smooth and homogenised. As the dough is rather sticky, form small regular balls using a small ice cream scoop, dipping it in hot water between each ball.
- Next put the balls into a large bowl filled with granulated sugar. Rolls the balls round so that they are well coated with the sugar.
- Put them on a baking tray, covered with baking paper, spacing them 6cm apart.
- Flatten them slightly (up to 1.5cm in height), pressing on them with moistened finger tips, then bake them at 150°C for 12 minutes. The ginger snaps should still be slightly soft when removed from the oven.
- When they have cooled down, store them in an airtight tin.

# Brownies

These brownies can be decorated with two or three walnut halves placed on the dough before baking.

A brownie can be reheated in a microwave oven for 5 seconds before serving. For a slightly more sophisticated and richer dessert, serve with a scoop of traditionally made vanilla ice cream or Chantilly cream.

Brownies keep for two months in the freezer in a hermetically sealed freezer bag.

**Makes enough for 10-15 people:**

250g plain dark chocolate,
250g butter,
250g whole eggs
(4-5 according to size),
250g caster (superfine sugar),
25g pastry flour (3 tbsp).

- Preheat the oven to 140°C.
- Roughly chop the chocolate into pieces. Transfer to a medium-sized pan with the butter. Heat in a bain-marie, in simmering water, until the two ingredients have melted. Mix well. Transfer to a large bowl.
- Using a spatula, add the sieved flour and the sugar, mixed together beforehand. Add the whole eggs and mix. Leave to rest for 30 minutes.
- Place in small individual moulds covered with a paper cup, either the ready-made commercially available variety or home-made from baking paper. Bake at 140°C for 25 minutes (60-70g) brownies or for 35 minutes (90-120g brownies). As the butter and chocolate content of these brownies is very high, they keep perfectly for a week if stored in a metal tin at room temperature.

# Green tea,
## ginger and mung bean patties

Bean sprouts come from the grains of two legumes: yellow soy (Glycina max) and green soy (Vigna radiata), which are called mung beans.

The green soy is a small, round green bean that can be eaten raw. Boiled mung beans are often used in Chinese cooking.

**Makes 12:**

225g dried beans,
600ml water,
250g flour,
225g soy yogurt,
200g soy milk,
200g agave syrup,
30g fresh ginger,
10g green tea powder (Matcha),
1 tsp baking soda,
1 tsp baking powder,
pinch of salt.

- In a covered pot, simmer the beans in 600 ml of water for an hour. Allow the beans to cool and weigh out 650g of cooked beans.
- Preheat the oven to 150°C.
- In a large mixing bowl, mix the flour, baking soda, baking powder, green tea and salt. Set aside.
- Finely chop the ginger.
- In a separate bowl, mix together the yogurt, soy milk, agave syrup and chopped ginger.
- Pour the liquid mixture into the flour and mix to a smooth paste with a spatula. Fold in the cooked beans.
- Lightly grease 12 small round non-stick pans and fill to the brim with the mixture.
- Place the pans in the oven and bake for 10-12 minutes.
- Allow the patties to cool in the pans for five minutes before turning them out onto a cooling rack.

# Pain d'épices (Gingerbread)

The mix of spices in this traditional recipe varies. However, powdered ginger is invariably used – and sometimes nutmeg.

**serves 12:**
500g rye flour,
500g honey,
35cl water,
1 heaped tsp bicarbonate of soda,
1 tsp ground aniseed,
1 tsp ground cinnamon,
1/2 tsp crushed clove,
butter.

• Preheat the oven to 180°C.
• Mix flour and spices in a bowl. Put the water into a pan and bring to the boil. Remove from the heat and dissolve the honey in the water.
• Pour this hot mixture onto the flour and the spices.
• Mix immediately until a smooth paste forms.
• Grease a 1kg loaf tin (pan) and pour the mixture into it. Bake at 160-180°C for approximately 1 hour.

# Manhattan choc chip cookies

**Makes 8:**

185g chilled butter,
125g caster (superfine) sugar,
125g light-coloured
soft brown sugar,
270g pastry flour,
3g salt (1/2 tsp),
3g bicarbonate of soda
(1/2 tsp),
1 whole egg,
1 egg yolk,
1/2 tsp natural vanilla extract,
250g plain dark chocolate
chips

- Preheat the oven to 150°C.
- Put the butter, caster sugar, soft brown sugar, flour, salt and bicarbonate of soda in a food processor bowl with the paddle attachment. Blend for 1 minute to produce a mixture of the consistency of fine sand. Add the eggs and the vanilla extract. Blend for 20 seconds.
- When the mixture is smooth and homogenous, add the chocolate chips. To bake, weigh out 110-120g balls of dough. Place on trays covered with parchment. Flatten each piece of dough with (moistened) fingertips to produce roughly regular circles approximately 18cm in diameter. Bake at 150°C for 20 minutes.
- If you are unable to find chocolate chips or drops, roughly chop a bar of plain dark chocolate with a knife.

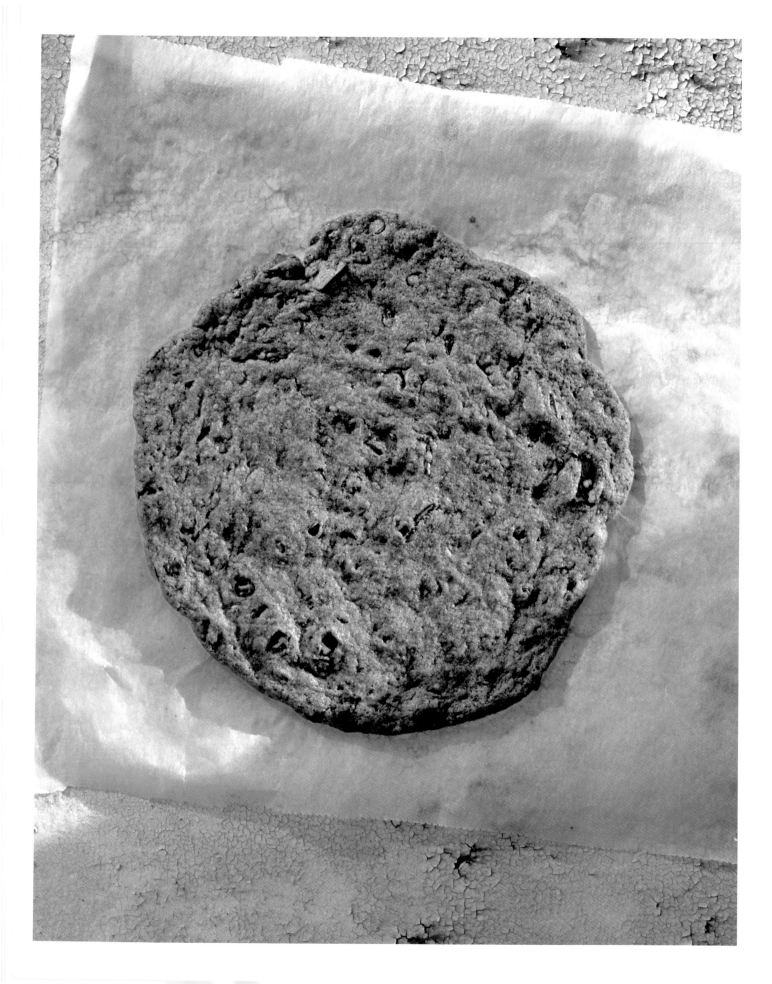

I had forgotten my car, which was parked in the street where it should not have been. Logically enough, it had been taken away by a tow truck. An hour later – it was already 9.30 am – I wanted to go and get my car back from the city's central police station, called L'Amigo, located behind city hall nearby.

No need to describe the atmosphere, with the waiting room, the desk officer on duty reading his newspaper, Le Soir, the newspaper par excellence of the French-speaking citizens of Brussels. Then I spotted the front page headline: "Give us our daily bread!" I could hardly believe my eyes.

Le Soir was talking about me, about Le Pain Quotidien! I ran to rue Dansaert, I dropped everything, the formalities and my convertible. At that moment, 25 people were standing in line outside the store. They were all there to buy *the daily bread*. By 10 am we had run out of bread. We suggested that customers come back in the afternoon. At 5 pm, we were there with 48 freshly baked, still warm wheat loaves. Many of the customers who had been disappointed in the morning came back to rue Dansaert in the afternoon, as we had suggested. And the second batch of loaves sold in 20 minutes.

Since then, we have always been rushed off our feet, '7 days a week, 365 days a year' …

# Fromage blanc, radish and spring onion (scallion) tartine

Farmhouse fromage blanc, which still goes by the name of maquée in Belgium, can be replaced by ricotta from Italy or brousse de brebis (a very soft sheep's milk cheese) from France. If necessary, it may be strained through a sieve or muslin an hour in advance, then kept chilled.

This tartine is certainly the one which inspired me to create these open sandwiches. One of the places where it is traditionally served is the Marolles district, the most authentic and typical of the 'real' Brussels, close to the local flea market. Early in the morning, antique dealers and second-hand goods traders can be seen seated at tables, enjoying it with a draught beer.

**For 4 portions:**
4 large slices of sourdough wheat bread,
300g farmhouse low-fat fromage blanc,
butter (optional).

**For the topping:**
4 spring onions (scallions), finely chopped,
10 radishes, thinly sliced,
Guérande grey salt,
freshly ground black pepper,
whole radishes.

- Spread the fromage blanc on the slices of bread, which may be buttered according to taste. Cut each slice into 5 triangles. Arrange on the sandwich boards.
- To garnish each board, opt for touches of colour and freshness, such as a melon quarter, a few slices of cucumber with the skin, a sprig of dill or flat-leaved parsley.

# Raw beef, Parmesan shavings, virgin olive oil and basil tartine

Apart from fillet, lean pieces of leg of beef can be used. A slice of entrecôte (rib) steak, trimmed of the fat and membranes, is also delicious.

The Parmesan can be shaved using a potato peeler, a truffle grater or a cheese spade.

**For 4 portions:**
4 large slices of sourdough wheat bread,
fresh butter,
300g ultra-fresh fillet of beef (bought that day),
medium-grained grey sea salt,
freshly ground black pepper,
4 tbsp extra virgin olive oil,
10-12 fresh basil leaves,
80g Parmigiano reggiano cheese, shaved.

**For the topping:**
sun-dried tomato marinated in olive oil,
olives,
rocket leaves,
lemon.
In season, slightly under-ripe fresh tomato, i.e. just turning red or even slightly green.

- Slice the beef with a sharp knife. Use a flat knife or a spatula to spread the chilled raw beef onto the bread, pressing down on it so that it adheres to the slices of bread. Season with salt and pepper.
- Roughly chop the basil and mix it into the olive oil. Spread this mixture onto the meat. Then sprinkle over the Parmesan shavings. Trim the crusts at the far left and right ends of each slice of bread and cut it into 5 neat triangles.
- Finally, garnish with the rocket leaves, tomato quarters and lemon.

# Rocket tartine
# with viande des Grisons

This recipe is inspired by a combination which is common in northern Italy - bresaola (air-cured beef) and rocket, which is served as an antipasto, or on panini, pizza, risotto, etc. There are several types of air-cured and/or smoked beef from a variety of countries, such as Swiss viande des Grisons, often prepared with spices, Spanish Cecina from León and Belgian filet d'Anvers. All these types of beef go well with rocket.

**For 4 portions:**
4 slices of sourdough wheat bread,
4-6 thin strips of sun-dried tomatoes,
8 tbsp diced fresh tomatoes,
1 bunch of rocket,
20 slices of viande des Grisons.

**For the rocket pesto:**
100g rocket leaves,
2 dsp extra virgin olive oil,
1/4 garlic clove,
1 tsp salt.

**For the pesto:**
- Blend the different rocket leaves, extra virgin olive oil, garlic and salt in a vegetable mill. Add additional oil if necessary to produce an oily paste.
- Spread some of this pesto onto the slices of bread and cut each slice into five triangles.
- Garnish each triangle with 1 slice of viande des Grisons, diced tomato, strips of sun-dried tomatoes and 2-3 rocket leaves. Drizzle the rocket pesto over the tartine.

# Moscovite tartine
## with fresh goat's cheese and salmon caviar

**For 4 portions:**

4 slices of sourdough rye bread,
120g salmon or trout caviar,
160g fresh goat's cheese,
160g goat's milk (or cow's milk) yogurt,
20g butter,
4 tsp chopped dill,
freshly ground black pepper.

**For the garnish:**

1 small sprig of dill,
1-2 lemons.

- Butter the slices of bread.
- In a mixing bowl, combine the goat's cheese and yogurt to a creamy consistency. Add the chopped dill and three twists of black pepper.
- Spread the mixture onto the rye bread. Cut each tartine into 5 triangles and add a teaspoon of salmon caviar to the centre of each triangle.
- Garnish with a small sprig of dill and lemon wedges.

# Brie de Meaux
## and walnut tartine

**For 4 portions:**

4 large slices of sourdough wheat bread,
1 250g triangular piece of raw milk Brie de Meaux cheese right for eating,
50g of top quality, fresh shelled Grenoble walnuts.

**For the garnish:**

radishes, cucumber.

- Thinly slice the Brie and spread it on the bread, top with the walnuts, pressing so that they adhere to the cheese. Cut the sandwiches into triangles, arrange on the boards and garnish.

# Beef tartare à l'ancienne (old-fashioned style) tartine

This tartare can also be served on toasted bread, provided that the bread is removed from the toaster and left to cool for a few minutes.

Tartare 'purists' are free to add a raw egg yolk to this preparation if they wish.

**For 4 portions:**
4 large slices of sourdough bread

**For the tartare:**
250g lean beef (sirloin or rump steak) ,
2 tsp organic mustard à l'ancienne (old-fashioned style),
2 tsp Worcestershire sauce,
1 tbsp salted-cured capers,
1 tbsp onion, chopped,
1 tbsp parsley, chopped,
pepper,
dash of Tabasco,
4 tbsp extra virgin olive oil,
1/4 tsp salt.

**For the topping:**
pickled gherkins,
chopped parsley,
poivre mignonnette (coarsely ground black peppercorns),
finely sliced onion.

- Take the beef out of the refrigerator just before slicing it. The beef needs to be cold, as this makes it easier to cut. Using a very sharp knife, cut it into 6mm thick slices. Cut them into 6mm wide slices. Finally cube the slices.
- In a well chilled large bowl, mix the meat in with the other ingredients using a fork until all the other ingredients are well combined.
- Spread the mixture onto the bread and draw lines lengthwise using a fork. Cut into triangles and arrange on sandwich boards.
- Serve with crunchy gherkins and the onion, parsley, pepper and caper garnish

# Pot-boiled
## curried chicken salad with date and harissa chutney tartine

Cooking a chicken in stock means that the fat can be skimmed off and is thus one of the best ways of obtaining very lean poultry meat.

This tartine is one of the most elegant solutions to use up left-overs.

**For 4 portions:**
4 large slices of sourdough wheat bread, fresh butter.

**For the curried chicken salad:**
300g chicken cooked in vegetable stock and chopped,
100g full-fat fromage blanc or thick sour cream,
100g mayonnaise,
a pinch of Madras curry powder,
salt,
40g onions, cut into small cubes,
40g celery, cut into small cubes,
1 tsp white wine vinegar.

**For the date and harissa chutney:**
100g dates, stoned (pitted),
50g hot water,
1 tsp wine vinegar,
1 tsp harissa,
pinch of salt.

**For the topping:**
a pinch of dill or chopped chives,
a few slices of ripe mango,
diced tomatoes,
crispy gherkins,
lettuce leaves.

- Marinate the diced celery, with a pinch of salt and a teaspoon of white wine vinegar, for 12 hours.
- For the chutney, marinate the dates with the vinegar and water for 10 minutes, add the salt and harissa. Pestle them in a mortar to obtain a smoothish paste. An alternative is to use a fork to crush the ingredients in a flat bowl or a soup plate.
- Mix together the fromage blanc, mayonnaise, curry and salt with a fork in a bowl. Blend in the chicken, onion and drained celery.
- Spread the mixture onto the slices of bread, added the diced tomatoes and cut each slice into 5 triangles. Arrange on the sandwich board. Garnish with slices of mango, lettuce and small gherkins.

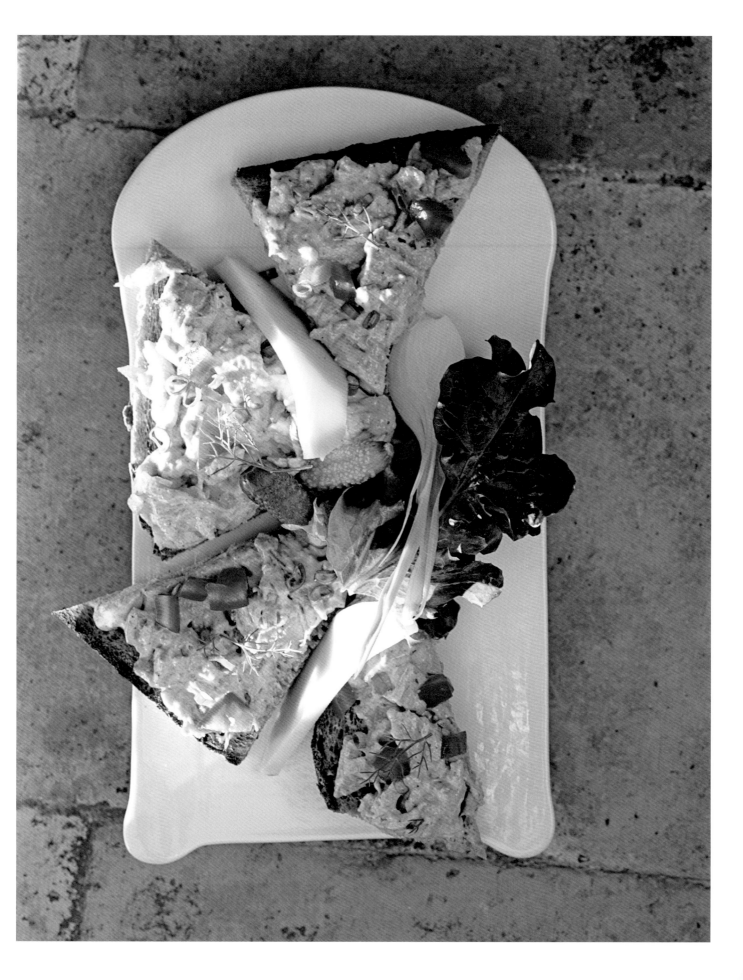

# It could only happen in Belgium!

The idea behind setting up Le Pain Quotidien was to bake sourdough wheat bread, in the form of 2kg round loaves, to sell them at the counter and to offer a simple snack bar service based on sandwiches, 7 days a week, from 7 am to 7 pm. Three or four days after the bakery opened, customers asked us for rye bread. It was also made using sourdough yeast and sold in the form of 2kg round loaves. One thing led to another and we started making a 1kg wheat loaf with walnuts. Then came 100g rolls, made with the wheat bread dough.

It also became apparent that croissants needed to be served with our breakfasts. But I wasn't equipped to bake them. For five or six weeks, we bought them from Nihoul, one of the leading bakeries and patisseries in Brussels at the time. The manager of our rue Dansaert store lived in the district where Nihoul was located. On his way to work in the morning, he collected our order of two or three dozen croissants and the same number of pains au chocolat and brought them by taxi. This situation quickly became unmanageable.

That was when we started working with Max. It was just a regular bakery and patisserie, nothing out of the ordinary, in a district near avenue Louise and Bois de la Cambre, a district in the south of the city. But in my eyes, Max was a champion croissant-maker. He had brought back an excellent recipe, passed on to him by one of his colleagues based on the Côte d'Azur. Every year, Max went on vacation to the south of France, somewhere near Cannes, and instead of just lying on the beach, he had asked his baker colleague whether he could spend some time working in his laboratory. Max's croissants were therefore very good. They smelt of butter. The pastry was nice and elastic. Even when the weather was damp his croissants were still as crispy and wonderful.

Our range of products remained unchanged for quite some time. It was extended when our 'production facilities' moved from the back of the garage in Anderlecht to a bake house worthy of the name, in rue de la Poudrière, a few hundred metres from rue Dansaert. At this stage, the story needs to be told from two angles: the production angle and the sales angle.

On the sales side, we got off to a flying start. We got unanimous support from the press, which described Le Pain Quotidien as something of a 'lifestyle' phenomenon. It was not very long before a first 'cloning' request arrived. Two weeks after the opening, in early November 1990, a lady called me. She was one of the very first customers. Her name was Evelyne Gérard and what she said to me in substance was: "Your bread reminds me of the bread made by the Madranges bakery which we eat every summer when we are on vacation the Ardèche département in the south of France." She clearly liked this bread.

Her husband had just been made redundant by his employer, IBM. There were mass redundancies at the Belgian branch of IBM at the time. The company's planned redundancy programme (compulsory under Belgian law) included work placements allowing future jobless employees to explore other possible occupations. Apparently, IBM took the view that small-scale catering (meaning snack bars) was a booming sector.

We arranged to meet, talked a bit, then they said to me in so many words: "If we build a store which looks like yours, will you agree to sell us your bread?"

The idea of franchising Le Pain Quotidien was born. One of the clients of my accountant at the time was a franchisee of the Phildar knitting wools network. He got me a copy of one of their franchise contracts. I typed it out, substituting 'loaves of bread' for 'balls of wool'. That was how the first franchise was agreed, without a legal adviser. I didn't have enough money – or at any rate I couldn't afford to pay a lawyer to act on my behalf.

In September 1991, the first Le Pain Quotidien franchise in Brussels was opened, on the corner of avenue Louis Lepoutre and chaussée de Waterloo, in the south of the city.

Chronologically, this store was in fact the third one. Once the franchising idea was mooted, other potential franchisees quickly came forward. The first Le Pain Quotidien outside Brussels opened in Ghent. The would-be franchisee had found a good location. Building and fitting-out took only six weeks. That was when we started to collaborate closely with Karel, our official cabinet maker, who has since supplied the furniture for all the new stores, from Los Angeles to Dubai. The table and the cupboards, for which we had hunted around, one at a time, in antique stores, for rue Dansaert, had now become standard, models that were set to be reproduced. Le Pain Quotidien spirit had been born. All that was needed was for it to be 'legitimized', so to speak. For the same reason, Norberte, the wall coatings specialist, and Daniel, her architect husband, were involved in the fitting-out of all the first stores.

In the late summer, I opened a store at Fort Jaco, in Uccle, a district also in the south of the city. I lived on the spot, on the second floor, above the store. I had started a vegetable garden. I had even brought an old glasshouse which had been used to grow grapes. It came from Hoeilaart, a small town not far from Brussels where grapes are traditionally grown under glass. It had been dismantled and then put together again, leaning against the wall at the far end of my yard. It was a very effective touch.

The store was smaller than the other three but as it was at Fort Jaco, one of the smartest residential districts in Brussels, where people are comfortably off, not to say rich, we sold 600 croissants and 400 pains au chocolat every Saturday and every Sunday, making a total of 2000 in two days.

The quantities required became so great that neither Max nor the two or three other high-quality local subcontractors who supplied us could meet our requirements. We were therefore forced to produce our croissants, etc., ourselves. That was one of the reasons why I transferred production to the rue de la Poudrière premises. Here we need to go back in time and look at how I had started out. I had rented the back of a garage on rue Heyvaert in Anderlecht, another district of Brussels. The layout of the premises was anything but convenient. As we made our deliveries in the very early morning, the garage was full of second-hand cars ready to be shipped to the Middle East or West Africa, the very same cars which were displayed in the street during the day. You should have seen us carrying sacks of loaves with our arms straight out, walking sideways, so as to squeeze between the cars more easily, for a hundred metres or so!

On either side of the bakery there were only warehouses and small workshops. The combustion gases from the oven were given off at the back of the building, behind which ran the Senne, the river which runs through Brussels and which, at the time, was more like an open sewer. There had been no environmental impact investigation. So I had installed my oil-burning oven, when I ought to have had a gas burner fitted.

This probably seems like a minor detail but it marked the start of my problems. My immediate neighbour, who had a traditional mayonnaise-making business, had just got divorced and had converted part of his workshop into a small bachelor pad so as to have somewhere to live. He was bothered by the smell of the fuel oil. So I got regular visits from the police. Their warnings, as much as the rise in sales, prompted me to look for larger and more appropriate premises.

So I found the rue de la Poudrière premises, with 600 m² of floor space. After renovation work and the fitting-out of an air-conditioned area for the croissants, pastries, etc., the first thing I did was to install a second oven. Once it became fully operational, we

# Tuna, tapenade and grilled sweet pepper tartine

Another way of removing the pepper skins easily is to roast them in an oven at 200°C for 10-15 minutes. Wrap them up in a plastic bag for a few minutes, then peel them.

**For 4 portions:**
4 large slices of sourdough bread,
200g tuna in brine,
1 egg yolk,
1 tsp mustard,
salt, pepper,
a dash of lemon juice,
6 tbsp extra virgin olive oil,
1/2 cup celery and onion, diced,
parsley, chopped.

**For the topping:**
3 tbsp black olive paste,
1 small sweet pepper,
mixed salad,
lemon quarters,
12 black olives,
4 thin slices of sun-dried tomatoes.

- Carefully strain the contents of the can of tuna through a sieve.
- Roast the whole red pepper over a gas burner (or on a barbecue) for 5 minutes. Skin it and cut it into strips.
- Blend the egg yolk, the mustard, the lemon juice and olive oil with a small whisk. Add the salt and pepper, onion, pepper and parsley. Finally add the crumbled tuna.
- Mix carefully. Adjust the seasoning if necessary. Spread the mixture onto the sandwiches. Dilute the olive paste with a drop of lukewarm water to make it more fluid.
- Draw a line of olive paste on the sandwich, cut into triangles and garnish with the strips of grilled sweet pepper.
- Arrange on the sandwich boards and decorate with lemon, black olives and herbs.

# Hummus
# with tuna tartine

It is always advisable to desalt capers before using them raw. This operation is not required for cooked dishes. Pickled capers can of course be used instead if preferred.

**For 4 portions:**
2 large slices of sourdough wheat bread,
200g canned tuna in brine,
extra virgin olive oil.

**For the tuna:**
4-6 tbsp homemade mayonnaise,
lemon juice,
salt, pepper.

**For the hummus:**
150g cooked chickpeas,
50g tahini,
1/4 garlic clove,
2-3 tbsp lemon juice,
25g mineral water,
salt, pepper.

**For the garnish:**
30g cooked chickpeas,
10 cherry tomatoes,
1 spring onion (scallion),
2 tbsp salt-cured capers,
a few lettuce or Batavian lettuce leaves,
a few chive stalks,
1 lemon.

- Put all the ingredients for the hummus into a food processor or a vegetable mill and blend to a fine purée. Ideally, add water gradually to control the texture, so that the hummus is more or less creamy .
- Mix the tuna with the mayonnaise. Season with lemon juice, salt and pepper.
- Spread the hummus onto the slices of bread. Cut each slice into 5 triangles.
- Add the tuna and garnish. Finish with a dash of olive oil.

# Red kidney bean and harissa cream hummus tartine

Black beans or cooked chickpeas can be used in this recipe. If you cook them from scratch, be sure to soak the black beans or chickpeas for the recommended time beforehand and only add salt to the cooking water at the very end.

**For 4 portions:**
4 large slices
of sourdough bread,
fresh herbs.

**For the hummus:**
200g freshly cooked or
canned red kidney beans,
1 tbsp fresh coriander,
2 tbsp spring onions
(scallions), chopped,
1/2 garlic clove, chopped,
juice of 1/2 lemon,
2 tbsp extra virgin olive oil,
salt.

**For the harissa cream:**
2 tbsp harissa,
75g tahini,
pinch of salt,
75g water.

**For the decoration:**
1 tbsp parsley, chopped,
50g tomatoes, diced,
thin slices of lemon.

- For the hummus, mix the beans roughly with the crushed garlic, lemon juice, olive oil and salt. Add the coriander and the spring onions at the last minute.
- The traditional recipe for hummus can be followed and the beans finely puréed to produce a smooth paste.
- For the harissa cream, whisk all the ingredients together for 20 seconds until an emulsion forms.
- Spread the hummus on the bread cut into triangles.
- Sprinkle with fresh herbs and add diced tomato and thin slices of lemon.
- Spoon the harissa cream onto the sandwich board, decorating it with a line of plain harissa.

# Egg salad,
## extra virgin olive oil, wild capers and anchovies tartine

**For 4 portions:**

4 large slices of sourdough bread, buttered.

6 hardboiled farm eggs,

6 tbsp extra virgin olive oil,

1 tsp mustard,

1/2 cup chopped herbs (1/3 parsley, 1/3 spring onion (scallion), 1/3 dill),

6 twists black pepper.

**For the topping:**

50 small salt-cured capers,

12 flat fillets of anchovy in olive oil.

**To garnish the sandwich boards:**

4 tomato quarters,

4 melon quarters,

gherkins, bunches of herbs.

- Slice the hardboiled eggs thinly with an egg slicer (guitar type), turn 90° and slice them a second time to produce a julienne.
- Place the mustard, olive oil and black pepper in a bowl, beat with a small whip, add the julienne of eggs and the chopped herbs.
- Mix for 10 seconds, taking care not to 'purée' the eggs. Spread the salad on the buttered slices of bread, divide out the capers and cut each slice into 5 triangles. Arrange on the sandwich boards and garnish each triangle with 2 anchovy fillets.
- Decorate with slices of tomato and melon, gherkins and a bunch of fresh herbs.
- Basil or chervil can also be used in the mix of herbs.

# Raw sardines and horseradish butter tartine

The sardine fillets can also be served with hot buttered toast or on a cress or rocket salad, seasoned with good quality extra virgin olive oil.

**For 4 portions:**

3-4 slices of sourdough rye bread,
2 very fresh sardines,
3-4 tbsp grated horseradish,
60g salted butter,
1 lemon,
4 dill stalks,
fine grey salt,
freshly ground black pepper.

- Carefully scale the sardines and wash them. Using a sharp knife, fillet the sardines and remove the small bones on the side near the head. Place the sardine fillets flat on a plate and lightly salt them on both sides. Cover and refrigerate for at least an hour.
- In a small mixing bowl, mix together the butter and grated horseradish with a fork. Set aside.
- Butter the rye bread with the horseradish butter.
- Cut the tartine into 6 rectangular strips and put the sardine fillets, skin side up, on top. Add a twist of pepper. Serve with lemon quarters and dill.

# Avocado, Nori seaweed and spring onion (scallion) tartine

The avocadoes need to be ripe but firm. Take them out of the refrigerator just before peeling.

**For 4 portions:**

4 large slices
of sourdough bread,
3 ripe avocadoes,
2 tbsp lemon juice,
salt, Tabasco.

**For the topping:**

1 tomato,
4 tbsp chopped bulbs of the spring onions (scallions),
1/2 cup julienne of Nori,
8 Nori triangles (base: 6cm),
lemon quarters,
slices of cucumber
and radish,
sprigs of dill and flat-leaved parsley, 1 whole avocado.

- Remove the seeds of the tomato and cut into dices.
- Place three peeled avocadoes with the salt, Tabasco to taste and a dash of lemon juice in a large bowl. Mash roughly with a fork. Spread this mixture onto the slices of bread. Sprinkle with the diced tomato and the chopped stalks of the spring onions.
- Cut the slices of bread into 5 regular triangles. Sprinkle with the julienne of seaweed.
- Arrange on the sandwich boards, decorate each sandwich with 1/4 fanned avocado, 1/4 lemon, 2 triangles of Nori and the bunch of herbs.

# Tartare of vegetables and tahini cream tartine

This tartare can be served as a salad with toasted bread. Smoked salmon or prawns (shrimps) can also be added.

Tahini is an oily paste made from ground and roasted sesame seeds (hulled or unhulled).

**For 4 portions:**
4 large slices of organic sourdough wheat bread, lime or lemon.

**For the tahini cream:**
100g tahini,
100g spring water,
pinch of salt.

**For the tartare of vegetables:**
50g julienne of carrots,
50g tomatoes, diced,
1 tbsp of the green part of spring onions (scallions), chopped,
50g red cabbage, grated,
50g green lentils, germinated for 3 days,
1/4 garlic clove,
50g julienne of celeriac,
1/2 avocado,
2 tbsp flat-leaved parsley, chopped,
Worcestershire sauce,
1 tbsp capers,
3 tbsp olive oil,
juice of one lemon,
Dijon mustard,
salt, pepper.

- For the tahini cream, blend all the ingredients for 20 seconds to produce an emulsion of the oil in the water. The same physical principle as a mayonnaise is involved.
- For the tartare of vegetables, chop each of them finely to produce a julienne, using a vegetable mill or a mandoline.
- Place all the ingredients in a large bowl so that they can be mixed together thoroughly. Spread the slices of bread with the tahini cream. Spread the tartare of vegetables on top. Cut each sandwich into 5 triangles.
- Arrange on a serving dish or individual sandwich boards and serve with quarters of lime or lemon.

# Duck breast
## toasted sandwich

As an alternative to black olives, black olive tapenade can be used, spreading it sparingly on the tomatoes.

To give the toasted sandwich an unusual texture and appearance, a waffle iron can be substituted for the usual one.

**For 4 toasted sandwich triangles:**

2 large slices of sourdough wheat bread,
50g smoked duck breast (10 slices),
40g grated Emmenthal,
1/2 tomato,
3 black olives, pitted,
1 tsp mustard à l'ancienne (old-fashioned style).

- Remove the crusts from the slices of bread, cutting off around 3cm.
- Place a slice of bread on the counter. Place the thin slices of duck side by side on the slice of bread. Spread mustard onto the duck breast slices.
- Add a layer of thin tomato slices (3mm thick) and sprinkle with the grated cheese.
- Thinly slice the olives and distribute them evenly.
- Put the second slice of bread on top of the sandwich and press down, cutting the sandwich into half.
- Put into a Panini press and toast for 1-2 minutes, depending on the power.
- Cut into triangles and serve with a seasonal salad.

# Chickpea with rosemary, roasted garlic and tapenade bruschetta

This dish, ideal for summer drinks parties at the pool side, can be served at room temperature. It can even be prepared in advance and then returned to the oven briefly before serving.

The freshly toasted slices of bread can also be rubbed with a raw garlic clove.

**For 4 portions:**
3-4 large slices of sourdough wheat bread, 15mm thick,
6 garlic cloves, thinly sliced,
2 tbsp black olive paste,
1 tsp harissa,
salt,
3 tbsp extra virgin olive oil,
1 sprig fresh rosemary,
300g freshly cooked or canned chickpeas,
1 bay leaf,
1 tbsp balsamic or red wine vinegar,
1 tbsp parsley, chopped.

- Soak 100g of chickpeas in water overnight. Drain, rinse and cook them in unsalted water with a bay leaf for 1½ hours. Alternatively open a can of cooked chickpeas.
- Fry the garlic and rosemary gently in the olive oil in a non-stick frying pan or wok for one minute. Add the chickpeas, the tapenade and the harissa and fry the mixture gently for 2-3 minutes. Deglaze with the vinegar, season with the salt to taste and add the parsley.
- Spread the chickpea mixture onto the bruschetta and serve immediately.

# Sardine, beetroot and lime bruschetta

If a toasted open sandwich, which is what an Italian bruschetta is generally taken to mean, is to hold together properly, the thickness of the slice is of fundamental importance. A thick slice makes for a soft centre and a crunchy crust. In addition, if the filling is juicy, a thicker slice absorbs the liquid better. That is why at Le Pain Quotidien we only toast slices that are at least 11mm thick.

**For 4 portions:**
3-4 large slices of sourdough wheat bread, 15mm thick, sliced with a knife,
2 cans of sardines in olive oil,
1 beetroot,
2 limes,
1 tbsp fresh coriander, chopped,
salt, pepper,
1 tbsp virgin olive oil,
1 garlic clove.

• Lightly toast the slices of bread and rub them with a raw garlic clove, according to taste. Cut them into pieces.
• Open the cans of sardines and remove them carefully, taking care not to break them. Set aside on a plate.
• Grate the beetroot into a fine julienne. Season with the juice of 1/2 a lime, salt, freshly ground pepper, the olive oil and the chopped coriander. Mix together well.
• Arrange this salad on the pieces of bread, add one sardine per slice and serve with quarters of lime separately.

# Wild green asparagus
## and al pepe nero Pecorino bruschetta

Small raw globe artichoke hearts or raw button mushrooms cut into thin slices can be substituted for asparagus in this recipe.

Plain Pecorino or Parmesan with plenty of freshly ground pepper can be substituted for black pepper Pecorino. But it would be a pity not to use this wonderfully flavoursome variety of cheese.

**For 4 portions:**
3-4 large slices of sourdough wheat bread, 15mm thick, sliced with a knife,
150g wild asparagus spears (or, alternatively, very fine green asparagus spears),
1 tomato,
125g black pepper Pecorino,
extra virgin oil.

• Wash the asparagus and cut the spears to 5-6 cm in length. Split them in half lengthwise, put them into a bowl and season with salt and olive oil. Cut the tomato in half, deseed it, then cut it into strips. Preheat the grill by lighting it or switching it to the maximum position. Cut the slices of bread into rectangular pieces, toast both sides under the grill. Cut them into pieces.

• Spread the asparagus salad onto the pieces of bread, finely shave the Pecorino over the asparagus using a truffle mandoline or a potato peeler. Place the garnished pieces of bread under the grill as near as possible to the source of heat and allow the cheese to melt for 30 seconds, until it colours slightly. Remove from the grill and garnish with the strips of tomato. Add a few drops of olive oil. Serve piping hot.

# Salted cod ceviche
## bruschetta

If salt cod is not available, several other firm fresh fish can be used, examples being monkfish, cod and sea bass. Other possibilities are scallops, giant shrimps and lobster – or even a mixture of them all. Naturally, all these fish are to be used raw.

This is a wonderful recipe to go with Tequila- or vodka-based cocktails.

**For 4 portions:**
3-4 large slices of sourdough wheat bread, 15mm thick, sliced with a knife,
200g coeur de filet (centre cut) salted cod,
1/2 ripe avocado, diced,
2 radishes, cut into a fine julienne,
lime (or lemon).

**For the marinade:**
1 lime,
1 firm tomato,
1/2 crushed garlic clove,
1 spring onion (scallion), finely chopped,
2 tbsp mixed chopped herbs (parsley, coriander, dill, small amount of mint),
salt,
1/4-1/8 jalapeño (small green chilli pepper), finely chopped (quantity depending on how hot it is).

- Soak the salted cod in water in the refrigerator overnight to remove the salt.
- Peel the lime. Dice it, using a sharp knife. Skin and dice the tomato.
- Mix these two ingredients with all the other ingredients in the marinade.
- Using a large sharpened knife, cut the fish into thin strips and place them in a wide dish with all the marinade ingredients. Mix carefully and marinate in the freezer for 5 minutes.
- Lightly toast the slices of bread and cut them into pieces.
- Place the marinated fish on the toasted pieces of bread.
- Add the thinly sliced radish and the avocado cubes.
- Serve garnished with pieces of lime or lemon.

# Hazelnut flûtes
## and Gorgonzola

**For 4 portions:**
4 grilled hazelnut
and raisin flûtes
(small and thin French sticks)
250g Gorgonzola.

- Halve each flûte sideways. Quickly grill each inner surface. Spread on 3-4mm of gorgonzola.
- This is an ideal combination of bread, nuts, raisins and cheese. It goes down a treat with a glass of white wine, made from Vendange Tardive (late harvest) grapes if possible...so likely to be from Alsace.

# Pain d'épices and carpaccio of duck foie gras tartine

To make it easier to cut the foie gras neatly, plunge the blade of the knife into very hot water.

It is important to choose a make of pain d'épices containing very little sugar. The optimum thickness of the slices is 7-8mm. Thin slices of toasted sourdough wheat bread may also be used.

**For 4 portions:**
8 thin slices of pain d'épices (variety of gingerbread not too sweet),
160g of very fresh chilled raw duck foie gras cru,
Guérande grey salt,
freshly ground black pepper.

- Use a very thin and sharp-bladed knife to cut the foie gras into slivers. Place them on the slices of pain d'épices.
- Cut the slices into triangles. Season with coarse salt and coarsely ground black pepper. Serve immediately as this dish is best eaten well chilled.

# Seared foie gras and cep (porcini) bruschetta

**For 4 portions:**
240g lobe of raw duck or qoose foie gras,
200g fresh ceps (porcini), washed and trimmed,
salt, pepper,
1 tbsp extra virgin olive oil,
1 tbsp shallots, chopped,
1 tbsp chives, chopped,
3 large slices of sourdough wheat bread, 15mm thick, sliced with a knife.

- Sauté the washed and trimmed mushrooms in the olive oil, adding the chopped shallot just before the mushrooms are cooked. Season with salt and pepper. Set aside and keep warm.
- Preheat the grill by lighting it or switching it to the maximum position. Cut the slices of bread into rectangular pieces, toast both sides under the grill. Cut the foie gras into 1cm thick slices. Place them on the bread under the grill as near as possible to the source of heat and sear the foie gras for 20-30 seconds. Remove from the grill and garnish the pieces of bruschetta with the pan-fried ceps. Season with coarse salt, freshly ground black pepper and chopped chives. Serve immediately.

# Whole cereal bread, smoked salmon and strained yogurt tartine

This preparation can be given slightly more 'bite' by adding 1-2 teaspoons of strong to medium mustard to the strained cheese. Mix well.

Full-fat yogurt can also be used in this recipe, as can soya (soy) milk yogurt.

I prefer mild smoked salmon because it is not too salty. Other smoked fish, such as eel, trout, swordfish and even canned smoked cod liver in oil, go well with whole cereal bread.

**Serves 4:**
8 thin (6-7 mm) slices of whole cereal bread (with or without gluten),
4-6 slices mild smoked salmon,
2 low-fat natural yogurts (250g) or 250g fat-free fromage blanc.

**For the decoration:**
dill or chives.

• In the morning, pour the yogurt or fromage blanc into a coffee filter and leave to strain over a bowl in a cool place (refrigerator or cold cellar) for at least three hours.
• Spread the strained yogurt onto the bread. Garnish with smoked salmon, cut into thin strips. Add the dill or the chopped chives. Serve with freshly ground black pepper.

# Whole cereal bread, pear slices, Stilton and traditionally made pear syrup tartine

Sirop de Liège is traditionally produced in eastern Belgium, in a dairy farming region. In days gone by, the meadows, the main feature of this hedged farmland landscape, were full of apple trees and, especially, pear trees with long-stalked leaves. Whereas other regions convert overproduction into cider or spirits (Calvados), a syrupy apple and pear concentrate has been produced here for generations. According to tradition, the syrup is made by reducing whole fruit, cooked in large copper cauldrons over wood fires, for hours on end. Production units of this kind are now very rare. And it is to be feared that some new set of regulations issued by European bureaucrats will put an end to this gastronomic tradition.

**Serves 4:**
8 thin (6-7 mm) slices of
whole cereal bread
(with or without gluten),
2-3 pears (Conference or
Comice), just ripe,
200-250g farmhouse
Stilton cheese,
4 tsp traditionally made sirop
de Liège.

**For the seasoning (optional):**
freshly ground black pepper,
jalapeño.

- Quarter the pear without peeling it. Remove the pips (seeds) and cut into thin strips.
- Arrange them on the bread, thinly spread with sirop de Liège beforehand. Add shavings of Stilton.
- Freshly ground black pepper or jalapeño can be added as seasoning.

## The Beverly Hills baker

Laurent and I arrived in Los Angeles on the evening of January 8 2001 to spend three days there. Le Pain Quotidien wanted to open in another American state, so why not the Californian dream? All things considered, it's more pleasant than Boston and its snow storms. Laurent Halasz had arrived at Le Pain Quotidien in early 1999, before the opening of the SoHo outlet. At the time he was working for a French investment bank in New York but was keen to leave his job to set up a Parisian sandwich bar franchise in the USA.

He came to see me because he was looking for a subcontractor who could supply him with bread. While we were talking I made him a dough whose texture I believed was close to his description of what he was looking for. Once it was baked, he tasted it and was literally bowled over. His French speaking partner had claimed that his manufacturing technique was a closely guarded secret and that it took time to become familiar with his baking 'technology'.

Laurent had no experience of the administrative side of a small catering business. He began by asking me questions about social charges, pay and insurance. We became friends and in the end I printed out for him Le Pain Quotidien's balance sheet and the operating account month by month. He was really impressed by the sales and profitability of the Madison Avenue store, the only Le Pain Quotidien outlet at the time.

We needed an injection of fresh capital to expand. Madison Avenue had cost $700,000 to set up. I had found business partners in Belgium. To open a second outlet, a similar level of investment was necessary, especially since there needed to be further investment in ovens. And to raise the funds required on the spot I had to have the accounts certified. While continuing to work at the bank, Laurent helped me to find a firm of experts. While they were tidying up our accounts, Laurent put together a sort of book which could be used as a reference.

Instead of paying for this work, which was considerable and highly professional and which I really could not afford, I suggested that he be given stocks. This proposition was agreed to by my business partners, including the new stockholders who, in the end, had been found…in Belgium.

Laurent resigned from his bank job and joined us during the first years of expansion in New York and in Los Angeles, where we had just landed.

It was the first trip for which I had made all the reservations on the internet: plane ticket, hotel room, car. We found a great hotel for $58 in Hollywood, the swimming pool was empty. On the first day, like any other tourists, we went around the local attractions. We saw Hollywood written in giant letters on the hillside, West Hollywood and its gay community, Rodeo Drive, the shopping Mecca in Beverley Hills, Mercado Central, which is 100% Latino, to name but a few.

Friends of friends, a banker and a realtor, drove us around and explained where the rich people lived, Santa Monica, the beaches, etc.

On the second day, we wandered around on our own, eating here and there, trying to get a sense of the prevailing trends. On the third day, we ended our search for locations in Beverly Hills. We were driving towards the airport when we came across what was to be come the first Le Pain Quotidien outlet on the west coast.

We were at 9630 South Santa Monica Boulevard. It was a brick building dating back to the 1930s or 1940s, one of the first in the city, so almost an archaeological relic in Beverly Hills terms. I looked through the window and saw the red brick walls, the high ceilings, their wooden structure, the garage style. Outside there was climbing ivy. It was perfect. The place was to rent, so I gave our realtor the telephone number on the notice board. Two days later he sent us a leaflet with full details of the building. I returned a week later to meet the owner of the property. We negotiated the lease, which was signed on February 1. We commissioned an architect, ordered the oven, the furniture and everything else. We opened on July 22 2001, just six months later.

Although this appears quick compared with the Madison Avenue experience, a great deal of time was in fact wasted. Planning regulations are very strict in Beverly Hills. It is not possible to choose the colour of the façade or signs, even the most innocuous things are regulated. Since the 1994 earthquake, all buildings have had to be strengthened, especially at roof level. All furniture has to be attached and cupboards have to be anchored into walls. To open four small windows on the side, three engineers had to be consulted.

Carrying out a construction project in Beverly Hills is a nightmare. No truck can be unloaded before 10 pm. We were even forced to empty the container with the furniture during the night. When we opened, we brought one of our bakers – a guy from Senegal – over from New York to lend our French baker a hand. We had rented a small apartment for him, five or six blocks from the store. So at midnight he had to walk let's say a kilometre to go and bake the bread. He only did it once. On the second night, a whole lot of police cars turned up. The cops jumped him, pinned him to the ground and handcuffed him. It would appear that it's not normal for a black man to walk around on his own at night in Beverly Hills. He was so traumatized by the experience that he asked to go back to New York immediately.

Besides this, Los Angeles being the movie capital of the world, we are still spoilt for choice when it comes to stars of all kinds. When Christophe Lambert comes to Le Pain Quotidien, he goes and has a word with the bakers to tell them the bread is great. But the star who is really fond of us is Jamie Lee Curtis. She lives in Santa Monica, but her office is located alongside the Beverly Hills branch of Le Pain Quotidien. She comes in at around 9 or 10 am. She adores our granola and even praises it in her interviews.

She's very approachable. One day when we were looking at the plans for the future store in Brentwood with the architects, she came over and asked where we were thinking of opening, suggesting other good locations.

Brentwood opened in March 2002, followed by Melrose in late June. Three stores in eleven months! Two were also opened in New York that year. Five openings in a year is a huge financial undertaking when you don't happen to have a millionaire grandmother.

Los Angeles gave us a different understanding of America. New York is a very international city. Consumers are sophisticated, akin to European gourmets. In California, people come to Le Pain Quotidien more for the decor and the atmosphere than for the food.

Of course, there are microcosms, like Brentwood, the 'street mall' of the people who live on the hill. When they get into their cars, it's the first place where they can find a few stores, where they can buy a pack of cigarettes, find a photo development lab, a hairdresser, a dry cleaner's, a little Italian restaurant where they can eat a quick snack. Actors are very much at ease in Brentwood, because buses with hordes of tourists don't descend on it. The day of the opening, Brooke Shields came twice, very cool in her little red jeep. The second time she realized that I was not American and spoke to me in perfect French. Dustin Hoffman also buys his bread there. He is very much into good food. I believe that he was also one of the Brentwood store's very first customers.

# Garlic and bread soup

Keep stale dry bread in a metal tin, taking care to ensure that it is moisture-free. This can be done by putting it on a plate and leaving it overnight on a radiator. Two weeks later, when the tin contains a variety of different types of bread (rye, spelt, sourdough wheat, etc.), it is time to put a good home-made soup on the menu.

The same types of bread, turned into crumbs in a food processor, also produce excellent home-made breadcrumb coating.

**Serves 4:**
200g stale bread,
8 garlic cloves,
2 tbsp parsley, roughly chopped,
1.5 litres water or chicken stock,
1/2 tsp salt.

**For the accompaniment:**
extra virgin olive oil,
Pecorino or Parmigiano reggiano.

- Heat up the water, bread (cut into cubes or sticks), salt and quartered garlic cloves in a 3-litre pot. Bring to a boil, turn down the heat and simmer for 15 minutes.
- Remove from heat and add parsley. Serve accompanied by good quality olive oil.
- A chunk of Pecorino or Parmigiano reggiano and a truffle grater can also be placed on the table, so that cheese shavings can be sprinkled onto the soup.

# One-minute
## sun-dried tomato and bulgur wheat soup

The combined action of the sun and salt means that halved tomatoes, from which most of the seeds have been removed, will become desiccated.

It takes 13-14kg of fresh tomatoes to produce 1kg of the sun-dried variety. Their flavour is very different from that of fresh tomatoes, being much more pronounced, more rustic, with a preserved, almost spiced tang.

**Serves 4:**

100g sun-dried tomatoes in olive oil,
2 garlic cloves,
75g bulgur wheat,
30g celery,
1 sprig thyme,
1 bay leaf,
2-3 tbsp extra virgin olive oil,
2 tbsp fresh basil, chopped,
1.25 litres water,
1/2 tsp salt.

- Bring the water to a boil with the salt, thyme and bay leaf. Slice the sun-dried tomatoes into a fine julienne. Chop the garlic and the celery.
- Add to the pot and allow to boil for one minute.
- Remove from heat, add the basil and olive oil and serve immediately.

# Barley soup
## and PGI Ardennes ham

This soup tastes better with a twist of freshly ground pepper. Black pepper or a mix of several peppers are best.

PGI (protected geographical indication) Ardennes ham is a raw ham produced by combining a limited number of operations. Salting (which involves rubbing dry salt into the pig's thigh) is the stage preceding actual curing, during which the future ham loses a proportion of its water content. The hams are then hung and left to mature in a cold atmosphere, reminiscent of winter, then washed to lower the salt content. The final stage is smoking the hams.

**Serves 4:**
160g pearl barley,
2 garlic cloves, chopped,
100g onions,
100g celery,
100g leeks,
100g carrots,
1 sprig thyme,
1 bay leaf,
1 clove,
2 litres water,
1 small tsp salt.

**For the garnish:**
2 tbsp chives, chopped,
1 tbsp lightly salted farmhouse butter,
4 slices Ardenne ham, cut into a fine julienne.

- Peel the onions and carrots. Trim the leeks. Cut them and the celery into 1cm cubes. Put all the ingredients into a pot with the lid on, then simmer gently for an hour and a half. When cooked, add the julienned ham and leave to rest over a very gentle heat for 5 minutes.
- Just before serving, add the fresh butter and chives and serve immediately.

# White bean soup
## and rocket (arugula) vinaigrette

Canned – ready-cooked – beans are ideal for this recipe and cut preparation time considerably. If you prefer to use dried beans, you will need 100g, cooked for two hours in unsalted water. Remember that you need to soak them beforehand in three times their volume of water, for at least 12 hours.

**Serves 4:**

400g cooked white beans,
1 sprig thyme,
1 bay leaf,
1 large carrot, diced,
1 celery stick, diced,
2 garlic cloves, chopped,
1.5 litres water, 1/2 tsp salt.

**For the garnish:**

2 handfuls washed and
drained rocket,
3 tbsp extra virgin olive oil,
1 tbsp red wine vinegar,
salt, pepper.

- Boil the water with all the soup ingredients for 20 minutes. Remove the sprig of thyme and the bay leaf. Remove a quarter of the volume and blend. Return to the pot with the unblended soup. Adjust the seasoning by adding salt to taste.
- In a salad bowl, add the vinaigrette to the rocket. Serve the bowls of soup immediately, garnishing with a handful of rocket salad.

# Maman Mahjoub
## potato and olives cassées soup

**Serves 4:**

300g waxy potatoes,
15 olives vertes cassées,
2 garlic cloves, chopped,
1 small onion,
chopped (75 g),
1/2 tsp dried cumin,
1 sprig thyme,
1 bay leaf,
1 small piece lemon peel,
1 litre water,
1/2 tsp salt.

**To finish off:**

2 tbsp extra virgin olive oil,
2 tbsp parsley, chopped.

- Peel the potatoes and cut them into 1-2cm dice.
- Put all the ingredients into a 3-litre pot. Bring to a boil and simmer for 25 minutes. Turn off the heat and add the chopped parsley and olive oil at the last minute.

# Brussels sprouts
# with cheese soup

In the north of France, extra-vieux Mimolette cheese is ready to eat after being left to mature for 11-14 months. It is an orange-coloured cows' milk cheese, its trademark colour traditionally coming from carrot juice, which is also used to colour Cheddar and Double Gloucester. However, Mimolette is harder in consistency, allowing it to be grated. In Holland, the other Mimolette country, it is called Commissie kaas.

Cheddar and other similar cheeses can be substituted for Mimolette in this recipe.

**Serves 4:**
300g fresh Brussels sprouts,
pinch of nutmeg,
20g butter,
1 onion,
1 sprig thyme,
1-2 garlic cloves,
150g potatoes,
50g grated extra-vieux
Mimolette cheese,
1.25 litres water,
10g salt.

**For the garnish:**
pepper,
60g extra-vieux
Mimolette cheese.

- In a non-stick frying pan, sauté the Brussels sprouts, chopped onion, thinly sliced garlic, thyme and fined cubed potatoes in butter over a high heat for 5 minutes.
- When they have turned colour slightly, transfer to a 3-litre pot. Add the water and salt and simmer for 10 minutes.
- Pour half the soup into the blender bowl. Add the grated fresh nutmeg and 50g of Mimolette cheese. Blend well, pour onto the rest of the soup and adjust the seasoning (salt and freshly ground pepper).
- Serve immediately, accompanied by a bowl of grated or shaved Mimolette cheese.

# Puy green lentils
# with Lapsang Souchong tea soup

Instead of a tea bag, 3g of Lapsang Souchong tea leaves, finely crushed in a mortar, can be used.

Lapsang Souchong is a smoky tea from Fujian province in China. Immediately after picking, its leaves are 'withered' over a fire of pine and cedar tree branches. This black tea is not widely drunk in China, being mainly an export product. Its smoky, woody flavour, evocative of liquorice, lingers in the mouth, leaving behind a hint of bitterness. It is a sophisticated and subtle tea which is low in theine/ tannin and is ideal to drink with a salty meal.

**Serves 4:**
150g Puy green lentils,
100g onions,
100g carrots,
100g celery,
2 garlic cloves,
1 sprig thyme,
1 bay leaf,
200g tomatoes,
1 Lapsang Souchong tea bag,
2 tbsp virgin colza oil or extra virgin olive oil,
1.25 litres water,
1/2 tsp salt.

**For the garnish:**
2 tbsp parsley, chopped.

- Sweat the oil, onions, carrots, celery and quartered garlic with the thyme and the bay leaf in a pot.
- After five minutes, deglaze with the water, add the lentils and the Lapsang Souchong tea, bring to a boil and simmer for 40 minutes. Remove the tea bag. Add the unpeeled cubed tomatoes and the salt, cook for a further 5 minutes, adding the parsley at the last minute.

# Beetroot (beet) and red cabbage Bortsch

The sour cream can be replaced by full-fat fromage blanc or strained yogurt. To strain the yogurt, simply put it in a paper coffee filter and refrigerate for two hours. Use 300g of low-fat or full-fat yogurt, i.e. three individual pots.

**Serves 4:**

200g raw red beet(root),

150g red cabbage,

100g onions,

60g celery,

60g carrots,

2 garlic cloves, chopped,

1 sprig thyme,

1 bay leaf,

1 clove,

2 juniper berries,

125g potatoes,

8 black peppercorns,

1.5 litres water,

1/2 tsp salt.

**To finish off:**

1 tbsp wine vinegar ,

1 cup spring (green) onions, chopped,

125g sour cream or strained yoghurt,

1/2 can tomatoes, cubed (approximately 200g).

- Roughly cube all the vegetables and put them into the pot with the water and the other ingredients. Bring to a boil and simmer gently, with the lid on, for 30 minutes.
- Add the vinegar and the canned tomatoes. Cook for a further 2-3 minutes. Adjust the seasoning by adding salt to taste and serve with the thick sour cream and the spring onions.
- The fact that Bortsch needs to be cooked for a comparatively long time means that the liquid may evaporate considerably.
- If it tastes too concentrated, you can add a little boiling water just before serving, in which case adjust the seasoning.

# Oat soup
## with kitchen garden herbs

The mixture of green herbs can be varied at will, using fresh thyme, rocket, lettuce, raw broccoli and young radish tops, to name but a few.

The same proportions of barley, quinoa or rice flakes can be substituted for oats.

**Serves 4:**

125g rolled oat flakes,
1 garlic clove,
50g parsley,
50g chervil,
50g spinach,
25g basil,
3 tbsp extra virgin olive oil or virgin colza oil,
1.5 litres water,
10g salt.

- Wash the herbs and spinach thoroughly. Remove most of the stalks so that 50g net (drained and dried) of each remains.
- Put the water, oat flakes, salt and chopped garlic into a pot, bring to a boil and simmer over a low heat for 5 minutes.
- Remove a quarter of the oat soup and pour into the blender bowl with the herbs and the oil.
- Blend for 1-2 minutes until the mixture is creamy and smooth. Serve the white oat soup in soup bowls and pour the green soup into the middle. Serve immediately.

## Flour and oil

When I first started out, I received 50kg sacks of flour. With the move to the rue de la Poudrière premises and, even more importantly, the increase in the number of stores in Belgium, we shifted into high gear. Cérès installed a storage silo for me and I paid it off on credit. But I was aware that the stone-ground flour supplied by Cérès was not the best available. And some of my customers, local good food gurus, told me that Poilâne's bread was better than mine and that its ingredients were of better quality.

So I went back to Lionel Poilâne's supplier, Decollogne-Lecocq millers, who were based in the Seine-et-Marne département not far from Paris. Apart from the obvious quality of their production, these millers were known for their organic flour. I asked them to supply me with it because 'going organic' was an ideal that I was already pursuing at the time. But they were unwilling to sell it to me. Thinking back, it was probably because they had too little of it in the early 1990s.

So we agreed on 'regular' flour and the deliveries started. It didn't last long. First of all, the logistics proved difficult to manage. They supplied between five and-six tons of flour in bulk twice a week, using a small truck. To make the trip between Précy-sur-Marne and Brussels cost-effective, they were transporting two pallets of sacks in the back of the truck. The exercise was a major challenge for them and there were occasions when I ran out of flour for a few hours.

Another problem was that my Belgian millers, Cérès, very soon realized that I was going behind their backs and obtaining bread flour elsewhere. Cérès asked me to supply them with a sack of the flour that I used. Two months later, their technicians came back with samples of really fantastic quality flour. They had changed their technology and adapted the grinding stones so that they could now offer me the quality I was looking for at a far more reasonable price. We worked on that basis until Le Pain Quotidien went organic. Their flour also supplied Le Pain Quotidien in the USA for a long time.

It was in spring 1993 that I met Majid Mahjoub and his family. The four brothers and seven sisters all lived in the centre of Tebourba, an agricultural area in the Medjerda valley, approximately thirty kilometres from Tunis. They are landowners and farmers. They also own a magnificent oil mill in the centre of their small town: a traditional oil mill with hydraulic presses dating back at least a hundred years and still producing first and second cold-pressed olive oil. Very few people still work like that today as the equipment required has simply not been kept.

At the time, major changes were occurring in Tunisia. During his 'reign', Habib Bourguiba had nationalized most of the country's key products, such as cereals, olive oil, cork and wine.

Majid's two older brothers, Salah, the man of the soil, and Abdel, the intellectual, had both studied in Belgium and were keen on the idea of exporting to Brussels, the capital of Europe.

The oil produced during the previous marketing 'year' – from mid-December 1992 to late February 1993 – was stored in tanks and venerable wooden casks. Raouf, the youngest brother and the manager of the oil mill, gave me my very first taste of a first cold-pressed extra virgin olive oil straight from the barrel.

Salah, the head of the family, the man who worked the land, then took us on a tour of the estate. He took us up to the highest point on the farm, a small protuberance in the landscape where the Romans had built an oil mill. It was magnificent! The crops on the farm were grown ecologically, and the farmers had a love verging on the religious for their nourishing earth.

Salah was also the manager of a local agricultural cooperative which processed the olives and produced mixed vegetables. His expertise was remarkable. His small niçoise olives and the green olives with fennel and candied lemon – which he nicknamed olives cassées – were quite simply sublime.

On each of our visits, we stayed at the family home, a square-shaped house with an unknownnumber of bedrooms. I'll spare you the details of all the varieties of couscous and tajines which the Mahjoub sisters prepared for us in turn.

I have particular memories of the kitchen where we ate breakfast, dipping toasted bread into soup bowls full of extra virgin olive oil. It was around that same oilcloth-covered table that we discussed prices and packaging.

By fall 1993, I was able to display Mahjoub  extra virgin olive oil, which I had selected and of which I was the sole distributor, on the shelves of Le Pain Quotidien. It was something of a long shot at a time when everyone swore by Italian oils, preferably from Tuscany, and people were not slow to point this fact out to me.

You come to realize that, with sufficient charisma, people respect your approach and follow the trends you  set. And Le Pain Quotidien was becoming somewhat of an expert in this area. This 'phenomenon' continued with sun-dried tomatoes.

I discovered them in a small Italian restaurant, a place atypical of Brussels, which I liked a lot and where I first ate mozzarella di buffala, which arrived on a direct flight from Naples twice a week.

I tried to obtain sun-dried tomatoes direct from southern Italy, but I failed to find the product that I was hoping for. Firstly, most are packed in sunflower oil. Secondly, to extend shelf life and to preserve the bright red colour, citric acid is generally added, and that was something I definitely didn't want.

That was how I came to think of the Mahjoub family's farm. They had no experience of tomato growing or of sun drying but they wanted to extend their range.  For the drying process, they referred to age-old sun-drying techniques. Thus it was that in the heat of early July in Tunisia, I found myself on the roof of the farm, where Salah and I dried the first tomatoes.

When the tomato drying process had been mastered, Majid Mahjoub suggested olive paste. I had asked him if he could develop a tapenade recipe. And he produced the goods. It is a pure olive purée, with a little oil. In the USA, several magazines adopted it as their favourite 'dip'!

Majid is always looking for new ideas. One day he asks you to taste artichoke hearts in oil. Another day he comes up with a sun-dried garlic purée in oil.

But Tebourba harissa is one of his most magical products. He has succeeded in giving this traditional Tunisian condiment an exceptional flavour, in part because of the way in which the chillies are roasted, giving them a slightly smoky taste.

Successfully putting some of the flavours and smells of one's native soil into a glass jar is perhaps the secret of happiness – although talent obviously plays a large part too. Since the mid 1990's 'Les Moulins Mahjoub' have made a progressive conversion to organic agriculture and now supplies Le Pain Quotidien with certified organic products.

I have always been interested in organic food. When I was 18, I used to bake organic bread at home on Sundays to take with me to eat during the week when I was away at school in Namur. I have always liked wandering around health food stores and I try to buy only organic products to eat at home.

I really had what might be called an organic 'revelation' after the opening of Le Pain Quotidien in Los Angeles. In California, organic food is part of a lifestyle and is often combined with vegetarianism. I have been told that a sixth of the population of California is vegetarian.

The sheer power of this phenomenon in California and the fact that it was mainstream prompted me to go and look for organic products wherever they may be found. It was almost six months before I was able to display organic bread in the bakeries.

First I reasoned in masses and volumes. Our biggest input was obviously flour. Several tons a day were used between New York and Los Angeles, meaning that we permanently had containers on ships sailing across the Atlantic from Antwerp.

American millers offered us very good quality wheat but none of them produced real stone-ground flour. Stone grinding produces flour which is far finer than that ground in metal cylinders. Bread made from stone-ground flour has the more pronounced taste of whole cereal and is crunchier, because the bran and flour particles are atomized better.

The conversion to both American and organic flour came about simultaneously, when I found a flour brand that agreed to change the way its product was made. It subcontracted milling to a flour mill in North Carolina that worked with stones.

For several months it was basically a question of trial and error. There was quite a lot of to-ing and fro-ing until we got the right grind, the one which gives our bread its character and its special texture.

Talking about organic products and foods, about protecting groundwater, bird life, etc., is all very well, but you can't claim to be saving the planet with bread and jam, whilst at the same time continuing to pollute it with milk and coffee. So going organic was a question of all or nothing.

That's how I found myself flying first to Chicago, then on to Madison, Wisconsin. After a night in a hotel, I had a three and a half hour drive ahead of me to LaFarge, which, with a population of just a hundred and located in deepest Wisconsin, I imagined would be a godforsaken place.

I had an appointment at One Organic Way with George Siemon, director of the Organic Valley cooperative. With almost 700 members in all parts of the country, this organic cooperative is the largest of its kind in the USA. All the farmers are stockholders, which in practice means that they are the masters of their selling prices.

Organic Valley sets the price of milk once a year. When you meet them they offer you a firm contract, protecting the producer and his customer against stock market fluctuations.

That was the sound basis on which we held our discussions and that they agreed to supply Le Pain Quotidien in both New York and Los Angeles with milk and eggs. And the arrangement suited me as my partner was a cooperative which had introduced a form of fair trade, encouraging sustainable agriculture.

I have pleasant memories of the day I spent in Wisconsin. The headquarters of this company, which turns over $300 million a year, are in wooden cabins, fitted with computers. The boss is a dairy farmer whose cattle graze in a pretty Wisconsin valley. He is a really nice and open kind of guy. We broke off our talks at lunch time and a secretary cooked wild mushrooms in cream for us.

I can't remember whether I started searching for coffee before milk. But the American way of life makes them totally inseparable.

Initially, we had served Lavazza, because they had helped us out when the Madison Avenue bakery and store had first opened. Afterwards I thought it was of fundamental importance to reinforce everything Belgian. For coffee, we used the Belgian coffee roaster Jacqmotte. Unfortunately, its taste was not geared to American consumption habits. Looking at people in the street, you would see them walking around with litre size coffees to go. One or two measures of coffee, even roasted Italian style, was not enough to give the required strength to such a large volume. Especially as tastes had fundamentally changed. Starbucks, a large-scale pioneer, had been the driving force behind the move away from the very weak 'dishwater' coffee, previously drunk by millions of Americans, to espresso coffee. Americans had developed a new palate, looking for bitter-tasting coffee. We didn't go that far, because we sought to preserve the fruit of the coffee, in the European tradition.

I remember that when I asked our usual coffee roaster to produce beans which I judged bitter enough, he told me that I was going too far and that my vision of coffee was sacrilegious.

Instead of responding to my request, he tried to make me accept his conception (at the time) of what coffee should be. And it wasn't strong enough for my taste. He probably believed that he was demonstrating something to me and making a point. But without success.

The main thing was to find organic coffee. We found an excellent partner in Antwerp, Belgium and opted for an organic Arabica hard bean coffee, offering us both a signature and continuity. The coffee comes from Villa Rica, a high altitude district in Peru where top quality beans are grown. Subsequently, we developed a range of organic teas with the same supplier.

I also worked on other products, such as dried fruit and nuts, jams, jellies, fruit and vegetables. We were still having difficulty obtaining regular supplies of some raw materials, such as red berries.

Meat, mainly hams, came at a fairly late stage in our research. The reason being that it wasn't easy. In the United States, hams from organically reared pigs could be found, but the processing was not great. I failed to detect the touch of the traditional pork butcher whose family had been in business for three generations.

In Europe, on the other hand, I made a marvellous find, a cooperative in the Ardennes region of southern Belgium which reminded me of Organic Valley.

They were pig breeders and sold fresh meat but also processed the pork into ham, slicing sausage and pâté. When I visited them in the town of Malmédy, I found a modern company that made a gourmet product using the old recipes of a small pork butcher in a nearby village, all in high-tech production facilities that met all the latest health and safety standards.

The pigs were very well treated—so well treated in fact that they were less stressed, which meant that the meat was of better quality. The cooperative – called Porc Qualité Ardennes – was also involved in carrying out in-depth work on a selection of breeds of pig whose meat is slightly fatty. This is important for the taste. I'm convinced that organic is tastier or let's say at least as good as the best 'traditional' products.

Le Pain Quotidien first went organic in California. There was not a lot of hype. Customers were informed via postcards showing a wheat field. On the back were printed the words: 'Bringing you the best organic products, we support sustainable farming for future generations'. And I firmly believe that to be the case!

Over and above principles, money was still the sinews of war. My partners had given me a free hand. But that's not to say that they would have accepted a decline in profitability.

I had done a great deal of work to secure supplies, cutting out middlemen as far as possible. But the extra costs associated with this type of agriculture cannot be avoided. So we passed them on, giving us a minimum safety margin. In practice, consumers benefited from all the work we had put in to find the products. We brought them organic products for the price of 'traditional' ones.

# Beverly Hills Cobb salad,
## with smoked tea vinaigrette

Dried beef or pastrami can be substituted for the 4 thin slices of jambon de pays (or bacon), in which case frying is not necessary.

**For 4 portions:**

250g cold roast chicken,
4 large handfuls of mixed green salad (young shoots), well washed,
2 tomatoes,
4 hard-boiled eggs,
1 avocado, ripe but firm,
1 scallion,
125g cucumber,
100g Fourme d'Ambert or Roquefort cheese,
4 thin slices of jambon de pays (dry-cured ham) or bacon,
dill,
flat-leaved parsley.

**For the smoked tea vinaigrette:**

10cl extra virgin olive oil,
10cl sunflower or corn oil,
5cl white wine vinegar,
1 tsp Worcestershire sauce,
1 tsp raw egg white (optional),
2 tsp lapsang souchong smoked tea,
2 tbsp mustard,
1/2 tsp salt.

- In the morning, prepare the vinaigrette. Crush the smoked tea in a mortar or grind it finely in an electric coffee grinder.
- Place all the ingredients for the vinaigrette in the food processor bowl and blend for 30 seconds to emulsify them.
- Set aside at room temperature for a minimum of 6 hours before serving to allow the flavours of the tea and the vinaigrette to blend.
- Slice the hardboiled eggs using an egg slicer: to produce a julienne. First cut the egg into slices, then turn 90° and slice them a second time. Set aside.
- Fry the ham or bacon dry in a non-stick pan over a low heat until the fat is crispy. Break the slices into small pieces. Set aside.
- Julienne the cucumber. Cut the cheese into slices, then into triangles.
- Dice the tomatoes and finely chop the onion. Thinly slice the cold chicken.
- Place the eggs, bacon, cucumber, tomatoes, onion and diced chicken in a large mixing bowl.
- Gently mix all the ingredients together and set aside.
- Place small domes of the mixed green salad in the centre of 4 large plates; spread the mixture of vegetables, eggs and chicken on top. Add thin slices of avocado and cheese triangles across the top of the salad.
- Garnish with dill and flat-leaved parsley.
- Serve the vinaigrette separately in a sauceboat.

# Scallion
# and Parmesan cheese tart

**For 4 portions:**
150g pie crust pastry or
bread dough,
24 scallions,
125g Parmesan cheese,
4 tbsp butter,
1 sprig of thyme,
salt.

**To serve:**
salade frisée (curly endive)
or lambs' lettuce salad
(optional).

- Preheat the oven to 160°C.
- Wash and trim the scallions, removing the root and outer layer. Cut them into 5cm pieces.
- Put the scallions into the bottom of a cast-iron casserole dish and add the diced butter.
- Season lightly with salt. Add 1 sprig of thyme, cover the onions with a plate and put the lid on the casserole dish. Cook over high heat for 1 minute, then simmer very gently to preserve the scallions, for 35 minutes. Be careful the scallions do not brown.
- Meanwhile, roll out the pastry or dough with a rolling pin to form a 20cm x 20cm rectangle. Cover the pastry with foil and put 400g of beans on top. Bake blind for 15 minutes.
- Lower the oven temperature to 150°C.
- Immediately spread the scallions evenly over the pastry and cover completely with thin slices of Parmesan cheese. Bake in the oven at 150°C for 10 minutes.
- Serve slightly warm with salad (salade frisée or lambs' lettuce).

# Mint and lemon
## taboulé

If you decide to use couscous instead of bulgur, be sure the water reaches a full boil.

Bulgur is generally made from hard (durum) wheat. This is cooked in water, then dried to harden the inside. It is moistened again, which strengthens its outer skin. At this stage it is roughly milled, removing the bran and the germ. Prepared in this way, bulgur has a long shelf life.

**Serves 4:**
50g fine bulgur wheat (or medium-grained couscous),
1 cup flat-leaved parsley, chopped,
10 mint leaves, chopped,
1 large tomato, slightly under-ripe,
1/2 tsp cumin,
10 twists freshly ground pepper,
1 pinch Guérande fine grey salt,
juice of one lemon,
1 cup cucumber julienne,
4 tbsp extra virgin olive oil.

**For the garnish:**
tomatoes, melon, watermelon, mint leaves, parsley, basil, coriander olives, lemon, extra virgin olive oil.

- Cut the tomato into cubes with the skin and seeds. Thinly slice the cucumber with the skin and seeds, then cut into strips to form a julienne.
- Put all the ingredients, except the lemon, into a large bowl and chill in the deep-freezer for 10 minutes or in the refrigerator for an hour.
- Take out the well chilled bowl and the lemon juice. Mix thoroughly. Mould the taboulé in a small bowl or a cup which has been coated with olive oil. Turn out in the middle of four large plates.
- Garnish with seasonal products arranged around the moulded taboulé: 3 thin tomato quarters, 3 melon or watermelon triangles, thin slices of cucumber, a few large mint leaves, olives, 1 lemon quarter, fresh herbs (parsley, basil, coriander, etc.)
- Serve with a good quality extra virgin olive oil on the table.

# Quinoa salad
## with grilled aubergines (eggplant) and lemon

Quinoa, a plant revered by and sacred to the Incas, originates in the Altiplano in the Andes and is reputed to be the world's most nutritional cereal. Protein-rich, its grain contains all the essential amino acids, including arginin and histidin, which are essential for babies. Another remarkable feature of this Chenopodiacea is that it is gluten-free.

Quinoa comes in the form of flakes, which can be used in soups or sweet milk-based desserts. The flakes are delicious cooked in soya (soy) milk, to which honey or fresh fruit can be added.

**Serves 4:**
200g quinoa,
2 medium aubergines (eggplants),
2 ripe tomatoes,
1 small bunch fresh basil (or coriander or parsley),
1 pinch salt and freshly ground pepper,
juice of one lemon,
4 tbsp extra virgin olive oil or virgin colza oil.

- Cook the quinoa in 4dl of water in a heavy-bottomed pan (pot), covered, until the liquid has been absorbed, which should take around 7 minutes. Leave to swell and fluff up for a few more minutes. Set aside the cooked quinoa, which should still be slightly al dente, in a shallow dish, in one layer. Holding them with a fork, roast the aubergines over a flame for 1 minute on each side. Allow to cool for 10 minutes, then peel them and cut them into 2cm cubes. Dice the tomatoes, keeping the skin and seeds.
- Combine the ingredients in a large bowl when the quinoa and aubergine have cooled down (to room temperature). Mix thoroughly but quickly so as not to crush the diced tomatoes and aubergine cubes.
- Serve at room temperature, simply adding a few a cubes of ewes' milk Feta cheese. This salad (minus the Feta) can also be served as a side dish with grilled meat or fish.

# Grilled vegetable salad
# with mozzarella di bufala

To save time, use ready-prepared roasted vegetables, which can be found in most deli departments (fresh or canned). Choose a brand without preservatives. Carefully drain these vegetables, preserved in oil, by leaving them in a colander for 30 minutes.

**Serves 4:**
1 large courgette (zucchini),
1 medium aubergine (eggplant),
1 sweet red pepper,
2 handfuls rocket,
2 mozzarella di bufala balls, 125g each,
extra virgin olive oil,
2 garlic cloves, chopped,
1 bunch basil,
salt, pepper,
2 tomatoes, cut into large cubes,
fresh thyme.

**For the accompaniment:**
lemon and balsamic vinegar.

- Cut the aubergine and courgette into thin (2-3mm) slices length-wise. Preheat a clean cast-iron grill at maximum temperature for 10 minutes. Mark the slices of vegetable by criss-crossing them at an angle of 90° half-way through cooking. Allow 2 minutes for each side.
- Place in a large dish and season with salt, pepper, fresh thyme, olive oil and garlic.
- Holding it with a fork, roast the pepper over a flame for 1 minute on each side, so that it can be peeled. Marinate with the courgette and aubergine for 30 minutes.
- Season the rocket with salt, pepper and olive oil. Arrange the rocket on four plates and divide out the marinated vegetables equally.
- Slice each ball of mozzarella into 6 thin strips. Place on the vegetables and add the tomato cubes and the basil leaves.
- Serve accompanied by a lemon quarter and balsamic vinegar.

# Carpaccio of raw zucchini with Caesar dressing

Serve this dish with toasted slices of farmhouse bread rubbed with garlic.

Canned tuna (100g) can be used instead of anchovies. Add 1 tablespoon of salt-cured capers and omit the grated Parmesan cheese. Blend the mixture to produce a fine tonnato sauce, like the one served with veal in Lombardy, for example.

**For 4 portions:**
4 small young zucchini weighing 150g,
1 tomato,
a few sprigs of flat-leaved parsley,
Parmesan cheese shavings,
freshly ground black pepper.

**For the Caesar dressing:**
4 anchovy fillets in oil,
100g yogurt,
40g fresh Parmesan cheese, finely grated,
1 egg yolk,
1dl extra virgin olive oil,
juice of 1/2 lemon,
1 garlic clove,
salt,
freshly ground black pepper.

- Place 4 large plates on the counter. Using a very sharp mandolin slicer, slice the courgettes very thinly, slightly cross-wise. Divide out amongst the plates in a thin layer covering the entire surface. Cover with cling film (plastic wrap) and refrigerate for at least 20 minutes.
- Peel the garlic clove and cut into 4. Put all the Caesar sauce ingredients into the food processor bowl and season with 6 twists of freshly ground black pepper Blend for one minute to produce a fine, creamy, lump-free sauce.
- Finely dice the tomato.
- Pour the sauce neatly over the courgettes, then sprinkle with diced tomatoes, Parmesan cheese shavings and parsley. Add a twist of pepper. Serve immediately.

# Feta, olive, spinach and sun-dried tomato quiche

**For 4 portions:**

200g pie crust pastry,

200g ewe's milk feta cheese,

75g pitted kalamata olives,

10 sun-dried tomatoes,

1 garlic clove,

1 egg plus 1 yolk,

100ml milk,

50ml fresh cream,

30ml extra virgin olive oil,

pinch of nutmeg,

salt, pepper.

**For the spinach:**

400g spinach leaves,

1 garlic clove,

1-2 tbsp extra virgin olive oil,

salt, pepper.

- Wash and dry the spinach. Heat the oil in a large frying pan with a garlic clove. When the garlic clove starts to brown, remove it from the frying pan and add the spinach. Stir for 2 minutes using a wooden spoon. Season with salt and pepper. Transfer the spinach to a sieve and drain. Set aside.
- Preheat the oven to 160°C.
- Line a pan, approximately 20cm in diameter, with the pastry. Cover the pastry with foil and put 400g of beans on top. Bake blind for 15 minutes. Remove from the oven and take off the foil and beans.
- Turn up the temperature of the oven to 200°C.
- Lightly oil the pastry with 1 tablespoon of olive oil.
- Spread the spinach onto the pastry base. Then crumble the feta and sprinkle it over the spinach. Julienne the sundried tomatoes and quarter the olives, then evenly scatter them over the spinach.
- In a mixing bowl, whip the milk, cream, the remainder of the olive oil, whole egg and the egg yolk. Chop a garlic clove and add it to the mixture, seasoning with salt, pepper and a pinch of nutmeg.
- Carefully pour the mixture onto the quiche shell and bake at 200°C for 20 minutes.
- Remove from the oven and leave to rest for 10 minutes before serving.

# M'hamsa salad
## with sun-dried tomatoes and fresh mint

The Mahjoub family is very proud of this m'hamsa (pronounced 'hamsa'), a typically Tunisian variety of coarse-grained couscous. Produced entirely by hand, it is made from hard (durum) wheat semolina, salt and extra virgin olive oil. The secret of its unique taste, texture and flavour lies in natural slow drying. From the purely practical viewpoint, it is cooked like pasta.

In Tebourba, it forms part of a traditional dish. It is served hot, with small pieces of dried and smoked mutton. Seasoned with home-made spices.

M'hamsa can be eaten like pasta with a main dish But it also ideal in easy to prepare 'one-pot' meals, for the whole family. This salad can be adapted and supplemented as the mood takes you, with tomatoes, parsley, coriander, olives, artichokes and so on.

**Serves 4-6:**
500g Tebourba m'hamsa,
7dl spring water,
10g salt,
20 pieces sun-dried tomatoes in oil,
20 leaves fresh mint,
extra virgin olive oil.

- Bring the water and salt to a boil in a medium-sized pan. Sprinkle the m'hamsa into the boiling water. Using a wooden spoon, mix gently so that the grains are evenly distributed in the liquid.
- Cover and cook over a medium heat for 5 minutes. Check whether the semolina has absorbed all the liquid. If not, cook for another 1-2 minutes. Turn off the heat.
- Add 2-3 tablespoons of olive oil. Cover again.
- When the grains have absorbed the water and olive oil, transfer to a large serving dish. Leave to cool down or to become cold, according to taste.
- Finely slice the sun-dried tomatoes and chop the fresh mint into thin strips. Mix well and serve.

# Spaghetti
# with sardines
# and stale breadcrumbs

Traditionally made harissa can easily be substituted for the chilli pepper.

When serving pasta with oil-based sauces such as pesto or aglio & peperoncino, try to cook the pasta for a minute less than indicated on the packet. Take a further minute off cooking time for more liquid sauces, mainly cooked tomato-based.

Semi-whole wheat pasta has a stronger, more pronounced taste, evocative of ripe cereals, than that of pasta made from white flour.

If you consider dry bread and canned sardines to be 'frugal' ingredients, spoil your guests with a good wine. This dish is full of character and a vintage wine will complement it perfectly!

**Serves 4-6:**
400g semi-whole wheat spaghetti (size no 5),
8 garlic cloves, peeled and quartered,
2 cans sardines in oil,
1 sprig thyme,
100g stale bread,
1 bay leaf,
1 dried chilli pepper, chopped,
1 cup flat-leaf parsley, chopped,
10cl extra virgin olive oil,
salt.

- Put the sardines with their oil, the garlic, thyme, bay leaf, chilli pepper and roughly crushed stale bread into a non-stick frying pan or a wok.
- Brown the mixture over a high heat for 3-4 minutes, until it is dry, using a wooden spatula to crush the sardines. Continue cooking over a very low heat for 10 minutes, until the mixture is golden brown, dry and crispy.
- Cook the spaghetti for 7 minutes in 3 litres of slightly salted boiling water (8g of salt per litre of water).
- Drain the pasta and pour over the sardine mixture, adding the parsley and olive oil. Mix together gently over a low heat, using two forks. Adjust the seasoning, adding salt and pepper and more chilli pepper to taste.
- Arrange in four hot spaghetti plates or bowls. Serve without Parmesan.

# Spaghetti
# with harissa
# and niçoise olive paste

Harissa comes from the Arabic word Ihares (to crush). Tebourba harissa, a speciality of the Moulins Mahjoub company, is of medium strength, enhancing the range of flavours of the dried chilli rather than its pungency. It owes its exceptional taste to light smoking of the chillies. A great product!

**Serves 4-6:**
400g semi-whole wheat spaghetti (size no 5),
8 garlic cloves, coarsely chopped,
2 tbsp traditionally made harissa,
1 tbsp olive paste,
10cl extra virgin olive oil,
1 bunch parsley,
1 sprig thyme,
a few fresh or home-dried oregano leaves,
2 tbsp salt-cured wild capers,
4 sun-dried tomatoes in oil,
salt.

**To serve:**
Parmigiano reggiano or Pecorino.

- Brown the garlic in half the olive oil for 30 seconds. Add the harissa, olive paste, thyme, oregano, crushed capers and sun-dried tomatoes in a fine julienne.
- Cook the spaghetti for 7 minutes in 3 litres of slightly salted boiling water (8g of salt per litre of water).
- Drain the pasta and pour over the garlic and harissa mixture. Finish off by adding the parsley and the rest of the olive oil. Mix together and serve immediately.
- Serve grated Parmigiano reggiano or Pecorino separately.

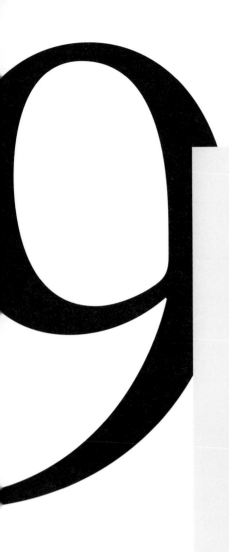

## Global and local

It is a long time since I stopped counting the hours spent on long-haul aircraft. True, these trips allowed me to collect air miles and to dream about using them for other flights to holiday destinations.

This 'global baker' status simply reflects a reality. Le Pain Quotidien brand is appealing to more and more partners and has taken us from Tokyo to Mexico, from Mumbai to Amsterdam, from Zurich to Sydney. It is now up to me to hand it over to people who, in their own country and in line with their own culture, will develop the concept, remaining true to the philosophy of the very first Le Pain Quotidien, opened in Brussels on 26 October 1990.

Each of our bakeries is more than ever a cosmopolitan place frequented by city-dwellers. Around the communal table we find regular customers who like the familiar routine and the comfort that they find near their home or place of work, and also feel a connection to the food and the setting in which it is served.

But customers of Le Pain Quotidien are also migratory travellers. During their travels they like to be reassured by a few familiar names and landmarks. And we are one of them. It is so comforting to be able to fall back on such points of reference!

For my part, these points of reference have always stood out and been as clearly defined as possible. The communal table, the bread shelf, the grocery products, the extra virgin olive oil and chocolate spreads, to name but a few.

The switch to all organic is another one. I see this step, which was initially objective, as a mission which Le Pain Quotidien must continue.

I like to extrapolate from ingredients such as flour, butter, milk, coffee, chicken, vegetables and eggs and take them outside the context in which we serve them. It is true that we work to promote consumers' health. But, translated into tons of wheat or gallons of olive oil, these raw materials account for thousands of hectares on which crops are grown using more environmentally friendly farming techniques.

The fact that the brand is now international has also led us to seek networks of suppliers where they did not previously exist. This leads to new encounters, which are always rewarding. The opening of the first Le Pain Quotidien in Mexico City, for instance, gave me the opportunity to visit organic coffee producers in the state of Chiapas. In Moscow, I discovered the extent to which the millers' milling techniques result in high-quality flour. The explanation is simple: during the years of food shortages, as much flour as possible had to be obtained from the same quantity of cereals. This meant that milling a few impurities in addition to the cereals was always welcome. In Turkey, I met stock breeders who wanted to turn their buffaloes' milk into mozzarella cheese, with the intention of becoming our suppliers.

This 'global' vision of the food planet, a chain that has become international, also enables expansion of the growing of local crops to be seen within the world of Le Pain Quotidien itself. France's great attachment to its wide range of varieties of cheeses is well known. It is therefore fairly logical that the French stores should have been the first to offer a range of 100% organic cheeses. The next step was to offer charcuteries (cooked pork meats) which are also certified organic. In this area, France acts as a sort of bellwether, proving to the other countries that sources of supply exist and thus providing them with an incentive to follow suit.

On the other hand, there are other phenomena over which we have absolutely no control whatsoever. But they influence consumer habits and as such are ultimately reflected in the composition of our menus.

For instance, in New York, it is a legal requirement for catering chains above a certain size to indicate on the menu the calorie content of each dish or beverage, including a glass of wine or orange juice or a cappuccino.

The impact of such a measure can immediately be seen in consumer preferences. To give just one example: our smoked salmon tartine – one of the most expensive in the range – has become a best seller, because of its low calorie content!

The USA was clearly a driving force behind our decision to lend our support to organic farming techniques. A similar phenomenon is occurring today with vegan food.

Just like organic food, the vegan trend came to light in the USA, emerging first in California. In some large cities, people who sit down at our tables are regulars, coming in several times a week. There are bound to be vegans amongst them. We therefore seek to offer several options in the menu, which as a result are also accessible to the occasional vegan.

I have found that this name is off-putting in itself. To caricature, being vegan is seen as a position taken by people who do not want to hurt animals.

The fundamental dietary principles of veganism are, however, interesting. From the strict public health viewpoint, it is clearly the case that we eat too many proteins and animal fats and that they have an adverse effect on cholesterol levels, for example.

Personally, I cannot contemplate giving up permanently a good local ham or a chicken's egg with caviar. On the other hand, I can imagine myself taking vegan principles on board during the week. You have a light and healthy lunch in the middle of the day; in the evening, you avoid animal products. But there is nothing to stop you from having a nice big barbecue at the weekend. You can also consider veganism as a way of detoxing your system on a one-off basis from time to time. Experiment with eating vegan – and raw – food for two to three days. The result will be almost instantaneous. You will feel like a new person and you will have a clearer head as an added bonus.

# Banana and pineapple clafoutis

This recipe can be made using only one type of fruit (either banana or pineapple). Low-sugar biscuits, such *as Petit Beurre,* can be substituted for bread. Small individual gratin dishes can also be used instead of a large one.

**Serves 6-8:**
3 bananas,
1 400ml can cocoa milk (unsweetened),
1 340g can pineapple slices in their own juice (or 250g fresh pineapple, peeled and sliced),
3 eggs,
2-3 slices bread,
150g fresh cream,
150g milk,
200g sugar or fructose,
peel of 1/2 lime,
juice of 1 lime,
100g grated coconut,
2 tbsp Rhum Vieux (aged rum) (optional).

- Preheat the oven to 200°C.
- Lightly grease a gratin dish. Cut the slices of bread (crust removed) into 12mm sticks. Distribute them evenly on the bottom of the dish so that it is covered completely. Peel the bananas, cut them in half lengthwise and place on top of the sticks of bread.
- Arrange the quartered pineapple slices around the bananas.
- In a bowl, beat the eggs and sugar with a whisk until the sugar has melted. Add the coconut milk, fresh cream, milk and lime peel and juice. Pour the mixture over the bananas and pineapple in the gratin dish. Dust with the grated coconut and bake at 200°C for 30 minutes. Serve slightly warm, pouring over Rhum Vieux according to taste.

# Apple mousse
## with cashew nut butter and honey

The cashew nut is the fruit of the Anacardium occidentale. Cashew nut butter contains calcium, iron, magnesium, zinc and B group vitamins.

**For 4 portions:**
400g organic sugar-free apple compote,
150g organic cashew nut butter,
4 tbsp acacia honey,
juice of ½ lemon,
pinch of ground cinnamon.

**For the garnish:**
75g organic dried apples,
verbena flowers (optional).

- Put the apple compote, cashew nut butter, honey, lemon juice and the cinnamon into the food processor bowl.
- Blend for 30 seconds to produce a fine mousse.
- Divide out into 4 bowls or 4 glasses.
- Cube the apples for the garnish and scatter them over the mousse.
- Refrigerate for 6 hours so that the flavours blend together.
- Decorate with verbena heads.

# Fig clafoutis

As the fig season is short, this recipe can be made with figs that you have frozen during the season. Choose small blue or black figs which are not too watery. Freeze them flat on a plate and put them in an airtight bag once they are nice and hard.

Vanilla can be substituted for lavender. Use a pod split lengthwise, scraping out the seeds with the tip of a small paring knife. Put both the pod and the seeds in the cream.

You can also flavour the cream with a pinch of ground cinnamon or, even better, with a cinnamon stick infused in the cream and left as a garnish in the dish when it goes into the oven.

**Serves 4-5:**
375g cream,
70g honey,
2 lavender sprigs (inflorescences),
4 egg yolks,
10 Petit Beurre biscuits,
12-15 small blue figs.

- Preheat the oven to 200°C.
- Break the biscuits into 5-6 pieces. Distribute them evenly on the bottom of a lightly greased gratin dish (or in 4 small individual dishes).
- Remove the small hard stalk from the figs and halve them. Place them on top of the crushed biscuit mix (skin side facing down) and bake at 200°C for 10 minutes. Meanwhile, boil the fresh cream with the lavender sprigs. Remove from the heat as soon as the mixture comes to a boil.
- Mix together the egg yolks and honey with a small whisk in a large bowl. Pour a third of the hot cream on the mixture. Dilute well and add the rest of the cream. Take the figs out of the oven and pour the hot cream on top of them. Return to the oven for 10 minutes, lowering the temperature to 110°C so that the cream cooks gently. Serve slightly warm or iced, depending on the season.

# Barley
## soya (soy) milk and roast apricots dessert

This recipe can be simplified by substituting apricot coulis for roasted apricots.

To do so, mix the fresh or canned apricots with a small amount of fructose and 1 or two tablespoons of water or lemon juice if necessary to liquefy the coulis.

**Serves 4-6:**
120g barley flakes,
8dl soya (soy) milk,
1 vanilla pod
(or natural liquid extract),
175g fructose.

**For the garnish:**
6-9 fresh apricots
or 12-18 canned apricot
halves (sugar-free),
2 tbsp fructose,
fresh mint.

- Split the vanilla pod lengthwise. Scrape out the seeds with the tip of a small paring knife. Put the pod and the seeds into a pan containing the soya milk and barley flakes.
- Bring to a boil and simmer very gently with the lid on for 10 minutes. Add half the fructose and cook for another 2 minutes. Add the rest of the fructose and cook for a further 2 minutes.
- Divide out the mixture in 4 or 6 small moulds, lightly greased to make turning out easier. Refrigerate for at least 4 hours.
- Turn out the desserts onto a large serving dish or individual serving plates.
- Heat up a non-stick frying pan and dust the bottom with the fructose. Immediately place the apricot halves side by side, skin side facing downwards, in the frying pan. Caramelize over high heat for 2 minutes on each side, until they are nicely coloured.
- Place 3 apricot halves on each barley cake. Decorate with a fresh mint leaf and serve.

# Pain perdu
# (French toast)
# with honey and spices

**Serves 4:**

4 slices sourdough wheat
bread (300g),
3 whole eggs,
1/2 litre tepid milk,
2 pinches cinnamon,
2 pinches cardamon,
2 pinches nutmeg,
2 pinches dried clove,
100g all flower honey,
40g unsalted butter.

**To serve:**

fresh butter,
liquid honey.

- Mix the honey with a pinch of each spice. Cut the slices of bread into 3 squares.
- Beat the eggs and the tepid milk. Add a pinch of each spice and leave the slices of bread to soak in this mixture for 5 minutes.
- Heat up two large non-stick frying pans and melt 10g of butter in each.
- When the butter is hot and frothy, carefully place 6 squares of bread in each frying pan and fry over a high heat for 1 minute on each side.
- Add 10g of butter when the squares of French toast are turned over the first time. When they are golden on both sides, put half the honey on the visible surface of the squares.
- Turn over and fry over a very high heat to caramelize. Add half the honey to the second visible surface and turn over to caramelise, still over a very high heat. Serve the French toast hot, with fresh butter and liquid honey separately, acacia honey, for example

# Granola parfait

The interesting thing about this breakfast dish is the contrast between the crunchiness of the granola, the velvety smoothness of the yogurt and the freshness of the fruit. Soya milk or bifidus yogurt can be substituted for regular yogurt.

Le Pain Quotidien brand granola is made from a mix of cereal flakes, dried fruits and honey, all of which are toasted in the oven to produce its deliciously crunchy consistency.

**Serves 4:**
400g organic granola,
Le Pain Quotidien brand,
4 plain yogurts (125g pots),
240g red berries
(strawberries, raspberries,
blackberries, blueberries, etc.,
depending on the season),
mint leaves.

- Take a large milkshake glass with a stem and put a teaspoon of yogurt at the bottom. Add a third of the granola. Then add 3 tablespoons of yogurt and a second third of the granola. Finish off with the remainder of both the yogurt and the granola. Decorate with plenty of fresh fruit, adding a mint leaf as the final touch. Eat immediately, before the granola goes soggy.

# Granita of peaches in wine

**Serves 6-8:**

750g white or yellow
peaches, washed and
stoned (pitted),
100g fructose,
juice of one lemon,
25cl white wine.

**For the garnish:**

300g fresh fruit in season:
cubed peaches, gooseberries,
blackcurrants, cherries,
a bunch fresh mint.

- Put the peaches, white wine, lemon juice and fructose into the food processor bowl. Blend for 1-2 minutes until the mixture is smooth and creamy. Pour into a square earthenware or glass dish and freeze for 6 hours.
- Put 4 ice cream dishes into the freezer at least 30 minutes before serving.
- Take the granita out of the freezer and scrape it with a tablespoon, starting at a corner, to produce frozen fruit flakes. Half-fill the well chilled dishes and add a little fresh fruit. Fill the dishes to the top with the granita.
- Decorate with fresh fruit, piled high, and a mint leaf. Serve immediately.

# Pavlova

Adding vinegar to the whisked egg whites produces the delicious marshmallow texture inside the cooked meringue. Leave out the vinegar if you want a stiffer texture (and if you want the pavlova to keep longer).

When making the small turrets, don't forget to build up the sides to give the pavlova height as it tends to spread outwards and flatten as it bakes.

**Serves 10-12:**
9 egg whites,
250g superfine sugar,
1/2 tsp white wine vinegar
(or white vinegar),
1 large tbsp cornstarch,
2 tsp natural vanilla essence,
1 knob butter.

**For the topping:**
double cream,
berries.

- Cover a large baking tray with greaseproof paper. Butter it, then dust with cornstarch.
- Preheat the oven to 110°C.
- Whisk the egg whites until stiff, and then gradually beat in the sugar until the mixture is thick and shiny. Add the vanilla and vinegar, being careful not to overbeat.
- Spoon the meringue onto the tray, making a dozen small turrets.
- Bake in the oven for at least 2 hours.
- Place on a rack and leave to cool.
- Serve with very cold double cream and the berries of your choice.

# Index of recipes

## Salads & pasta

## Soups

## Tartines